Joyful Unity in the Gospel (The Call of Philippians)

by A. Blake White

A. Blake White, Joyful Unity in the Gospel (The Call of Philippians)

Copyright © 2015 by A. Blake White

Published by Cross to Crown Ministries
5210 Centennial Blvd
Colorado Springs, CO 80919
www.crosstocrown.org

Cover design by Daniel Davidson, Colorado Springs, CO | www.bydan.us

Printed in the United States of America

ISBN: 978-0-9851187-7-8

To Momz,

Thanks for being a prayer warrior and encourager, and when necessary, the bearer of a gentle rebuke. So crucial to all I do. Thanks for teaching me to work sacrificially, love hard, and laugh loud. Love you very much.

"I thank my God every time I remember you."

Contents

Other Books by A. Blake White by A. Blake White:

The Newness of the New Covenant
The Law of Christ: A Theological Proposal
Galatians: A Theological Interpretation
Abide in Him: A Theological Interpretation of John's First Letter
Union with Christ: Last Adam and Seed of Abraham
What Is New Covenant Theology? An Introduction
Theological Foundations for New Covenant Ethics
The Abrahamic Promises in Galatians
Missional Ecclesiology
The Imitation of Jesus

[1]

Joyful Unity in the Gospel

Everyone loves the book of Philippians. Rightly so. It is short, sweet, and full of gospel truth and rich application.

But what is the backstory? Why did Paul write it? Who was he writing to? The answer begins in the book of Acts. After seeing a vision of a distressed man calling to him from Macedonia (Acts 16:9-10), Paul continued his missionary journey and traveled to Philippi. There he confronted several different kinds of people with the message of grace, as F.F. Bruce writes,

> Three individuals are singled out by Luke among those whose lives were influenced for good by the gospel at Philippi; they differ so much one from another that he might be thought to have selected them deliberately in order to show how the saving power of the name of Jesus was shown in the most diverse types of men and women.[1]

These individuals included a female business owner, a slave girl, and a prison guard. Here is the entire account:

> *During the night a vision appeared to Paul: A Macedonian man was standing and pleading with him, "Cross over to Macedonia and help us!" After he had seen the vision, we immediately made efforts to set out for Macedonia, concluding that God had called us to evangelize them.*

Then, setting sail from Troas, we ran a straight course to Samothrace, the next day to Neapolis, and from there to Philippi...On the Sabbath day we went outside the city gate by the river, where we thought there was a place of prayer. We sat down and spoke to the women gathered there. A woman named Lydia, a dealer in purple cloth from the city of Thyatira, who worshiped God, was listening. The Lord opened her heart to pay attention to what was spoken by Paul. After she and her household were baptized, she urged us, "If you consider me a believer in the Lord, come and stay at my house." And she persuaded us.

Once, as we were on our way to prayer, a slave girl met us who had a spirit of prediction. She made a large profit for her owners by fortune-telling. As she followed Paul and us she cried out, "These men, who are proclaiming to you the way of salvation, are the slaves of the Most High God." And she did this for many days.

But Paul was greatly aggravated and turning to the spirit, said, "I command you in the name of Jesus Christ to come out of her!" And it came out right away.

When her owners saw that their hope of profit was gone, they seized Paul and Silas and dragged them into the marketplace to the authorities. Bringing them before the chief magistrates, they said, "These men are seriously disturbing our city. They are Jews and are promoting customs that are not legal for us as Romans to adopt or practice."

Then the mob joined in the attack against them, and the chief magistrates stripped off their clothes and ordered them to be beaten with rods. After they had inflicted many blows on them, they threw them in jail, ordering the jailer to keep them securely guarded. Receiving such an order, he put them into the inner prison and secured their feet in the stocks.

About midnight Paul and Silas were praying and singing hymns to God, and the prisoners were listening to them. Suddenly there was such a violent earthquake that the foundations of the jail were shaken, and immediately all the doors were opened, and everyone's chains came loose. When the jailer woke up and saw the doors of the prison open, he drew his sword and was going to kill himself, since he thought the prisoners had escaped.

But Paul called out in a loud voice, "Don't harm yourself, because all of us are here!"

Then the jailer called for lights, rushed in, and fell down trembling before Paul and Silas. Then he escorted them out and said, "Sirs, what must I do to be saved?"

So they said, "Believe on the Lord Jesus, and you will be saved—you and your household." Then they spoke the message of the Lord to him along with everyone in his house. He took them the same hour of the night and washed their wounds. Right away he and all his family were baptized. He brought them into his house, set a meal before them, and rejoiced because he had believed God with his entire household." (Acts 16:9-34)

An Enterprising Woman

Paul usually began his missionary work at the local Jewish synagogue, but there wasn't one in Philippi. Apparently, there weren't ten Jewish men in this Roman colony, the number needed to form a synagogue.[2] But there was a ladies' Bible study down by the riverside.[3] One of the participants was a woman named Lydia.

Lydia was from Thyatira and probably owned a successful fashion company. Her main clients would have been affluent people, since purple was the color the wealthy wore. On one providential day, while listening in on Paul's teaching, she learned to what, or to *whom*, the Hebrew Bible pointed – Jesus Christ. As Paul spoke, the Lord opened Lydia's heart to what he was saying (Acts 16:14).

That is grace, friends. Irresistible grace! Paul told her the gospel and God opened her heart to believe it. How many times did you hear the good news of Jesus before it finally hit home? In His timing, God opened your heart just like He did Lydia's. And notice how her life changed. Immediately, she was hospitable, inviting Paul, Silas, and Timothy to her house. She was quick to serve other believers and to use her resources for the propagation and advancement of the gospel. True conversion inevitably leads to a desire to see others converted.

A Demon-Possessed Girl

Next, grace grabbed a fortune-telling slave girl. She had been following the apostles around for many days, announcing to everyone what they were trying to do. Paul finally had enough of it and commanded the spirit to buzz off. And buzz off it did, frustrating her owners whose profits buzzed off with it. Paul and the others were dragged off to the authorities where they were accused of preaching against Caesar (which was partly true since they were announcing the reign of a new King[4]). They were stripped, beaten with rods, and tossed into prison, but the girl was released from her bondage to the evil spirit.

The Warden

Naked, battered, and sulking in despair, the disciples cried aloud to God – *Why us?* No, actually, they didn't. One would expect groaning and complaining, but instead they prayed and sang hymns.[5] As the 2nd century theologian Tertullian put it, "The legs feel nothing in the stocks when the heart is in heaven."[6] Their faith was strong. It was like an earlier time when the disciples were persecuted by the Jews, and they rejoiced that they were counted worthy to be dishonored on behalf of Jesus (Acts 5:41). They truly believed in the surpassing worth of Jesus. Do we? Brothers and sisters, we need to cultivate a faith that sings when trials come.

God miraculously freed Paul and Silas through an earthquake. Nothing can stop His mission! But when the jailer saw what was happening, he panicked. He knew that once his boss found out that the prisoners were gone, he would be put to death in a way far worse than stabbing himself with a sword. But as he was about to take his own life, Paul shouted and told him not to do it, that they had not escaped.

Paul was free, but risked his own life to save the jailer's. This theme of giving of self for the good of others — what I have called elsewhere *cruciform love*[7] — will surface again and again. Before he became a Christian, Paul held the robes of the Jews who killed Stephen for preaching Jesus, and no doubt Paul recalled that experience in the midst of his own suffering. Stephen prayed for the blessing of those who were persecuting him: "Lord, do not charge them with this sin" (Acts 7:60). Stephen was following the example of his Lord who prayed, "Father, forgive them, because they do not know what they are doing" (Luke 23:34). Here Paul could have escaped, but he was more concerned about the salvation of the jailer than his own freedom.

This jailer knew that the God to whom these Christians were praying and singing was the real deal. So he asked, "What must I do to be saved?" (Acts 16:30). The answer was, "Believe on the Lord Jesus." A simple, but life-transforming answer.

He believed and expressed his faith through baptism. Then he cleaned them up and fed them. Just as with Lydia, this man's faith immediately led him to serve God's people.

Paul's Message for Us

The Philippian church started as a motley crew, but it was a motley crew with a saving message. This shows that the grace of Jesus is available to all—the rich and poor, men and women, slave and free, black, white, brown, or green. Salvation is available to the demon-possessed, to the blue collar and white collar, to the tattooed and the preppy, to the Republican and the Democrat. *Whosoever will* may come: "For God loved the world in this way: He gave His One and Only Son, so that everyone who believes in Him will not perish but have eternal life" (John 3:16). The message continues to save, even today.

Just like Paul, we are integral to God's saving mission. The world is full of disobedient people who act just like the first two humans, Adam and Eve, whose actions brought sin and death into the world. But throughout the OT, God promised to send a Savior who would redeem sinners. That Savior is Jesus.

After His life, death, and resurrection, but before He ascended into Heaven, He told His disciples that they would receive power from the Holy Spirit to be His witnesses to all nations (Acts 1:8). They would be His Church on a mission to declare the good news of salvation and redemption. But it is not really the Church's mission. As one has put it, "It is not the church of God that has a mission in the world, but the God of mission that has a church in the world." God's mission is the reason the Church exists.

But in order for us to do our part in His mission, our community must be unified. We must walk in a manner worthy of the gospel. That is why *Philippians* was written. We need to hear its message and let it shape us so that we function effectively in God's redemptive purposes. If we pursue the kind of joyful unity that Paul wrote about, we will be a vital part of God's plan for saving the world.

Notes

1. F.F. Bruce, *The Book of the Acts* (Grand Rapids: Eerdmans, 1988), 312.

2. David G. Peterson, *The Acts of the Apostles* (Grand Rapids: Eerdmans, 2009), 460.

3. Matt Chandler, *To Live is Christ To Die is Gain* (Colorado Springs: David C. Cook, 2013), 18. Praise God for faithful women of God. Chances are you would not be interested in such things as the book of Philippians had it not been for the prayers and encouragement of faithful women. I know it is true of me.

4. Acts 17:7.

5. Bruce, *The Book of the Acts*, 317.

6. Tertullian, *To the Martyrs*, quoted in Bruce, *The Book of the Acts*, 317.

7. See Part Two of my *Theological Foundations for New Covenant Ethics* (Frederick, MD: New Covenant Media, 2013).

2

Thank God for Partners in Grace

Paul and Timothy, slaves of Christ Jesus: To all the saints in Christ Jesus who are in Philippi, including the overseers and deacons. Grace to you and peace from God our Father and the Lord Jesus Christ. I give thanks to my God for every remembrance of you, always praying with joy for all of you in my every prayer, because of your partnership in the gospel from the first day until now. I am sure of this, that He who started a good work in you will carry it on to completion until the day of Christ Jesus. It is right for me to think this way about all of you, because I have you in my heart, and you are all partners with me in grace, both in my imprisonment and in the defense and establishment of the gospel. (Philippians 1:1-7)

Owned by Jesus

Paul refers to himself and his partner Timothy as "slaves of Christ." Contrary to the way it sounds, *Christ* is not Jesus' last name, it's His title.[1] It's a *royal* title – Jesus is their King. Many translations soften the verse by using "servants" rather than "slaves," but there is an important difference between the two.[2] As Murray Harris points out, "A servant gives service to someone, but a slave belongs to someone."[3] Paul and Timothy are *owned* by Jesus. This is a common but striking way of describing disciples. If you are a Christian, your life is no longer your own. Jesus is your Lord.

Who Are the Saints?

Paul refers to the Philippian believers as "saints." According to the Bible, every Christian is a "saint" or "holy one" or "set apart one" (contra Roman Catholic doctrine which has confused the issue by only making certain special people saints). It doesn't refer to our moral achievements, but to our status in Christ. Simply by trusting Christ we are sanctified, which is why Paul could call the Corinthians, a church filled with moral and theological problems, "saints" (1 Cor. 1:2). Sainthood comes not by our holiness but by the work of God. Karl Barth writes:

> "Holy" people are unholy people, who nevertheless as such have been singled out, claimed, and requisitioned by God for his control, for his use, for himself who is holy. Their holiness is and remains in Christ Jesus. It is in him that they are holy; it is from this point of view that they are to be addressed as such, in no other respect.[4]

Leaders Who Serve

Paul singles out *overseers and deacons* in his greeting. The consistent picture of the Church in the NT shows that she is led by *overseers* (sometimes translated *bishops*)[5] and served by *deacons*. For example, Paul lays out the qualifications for overseers in 1 Timothy 3:1-7 and for deacons in 1 Timothy 3:8-13.[6] Later church tradition would develop a complex hierarchical system, but in the beginning it was quite simple – overseers and deacons, both given to serve the congregation ("all the saints") under the lordship of King Jesus.

Father, Son, and Holy Spirit

Paul wishes them grace and peace *from God the Father and the Lord Jesus Christ.*[7] For modern Christians, this is normal stuff, but it would have been shocking in the first century. Paul just placed Jesus Christ on the same level as God the Father! Philippians, like the entire NT, is Trinitarian through and through. In 2:1, Paul speaks of encouragement in Christ and the fellowship with the Spirit. In 2:9-11, he speaks of God the Father giving the highest name to God the Son so that all will acclaim Jesus as Lord to the glory of God the Father.

Be Thankful

The main verb in Philippians 1:3 is "give thanks." Everything else in Philippians 1:3-7 modifies it. Let's consider several aspects of Paul's gratitude.

To whom does Paul give thanks?

God. God is to be thanked for everything. Every good gift comes down from the Father of lights. Every. Good. Gift. Oh, how we are so frequently ingrates!

Becoming parents has taught my wife and me gratitude for our own padres. For example, my family does a lot of traveling. When it comes time for a road trip, my kids are exhaustion-inducingly dependent on us. They can barely put on – much less tie – their own shoes. My three-year-old is lucky if his shirt isn't on backwards. They wake up, eat their cereal, drink their milk, hop in the van, and wait for one of us to buckle them (since their mini-arms aren't yet strong enough to snap it in place). Then we go. And they immediately ask if we have arrived yet. I say, "No, buddy. Just put it in reverse. Sit tight."

What these little raccoons aren't aware of is how much work their Momma and I have been doing while they lay cuddling with soft furry animals and dreaming about trains. *Our* road trip started the night before: clothes, bath stuff, snacks, cups, diapers, wipes, Elmo, sound machine, Curious George, brown blanket, pack-n-play. We were up an hour before them folding clothes, packing bags, loading strollers, and skimming the check-lists in our heads. They think we all just wake up, and lo and behold, the van is filled to the brim. There's no "Thanks, Mom and Dad, for all your hard work!" No "Blessed be me for my selfless parents!" No "How kind of my parents to work so hard on my behalf!" Just "I need some fruit snacks! Then some goldfish! With juice! The red kind!"

The care of parents for their little ones is significant, but it's gnat-like in comparison to God's everyday concern for His creation. Independence is a satanic myth. Just think of how much we rely on the omni-generous God at all times. He sustains the chair you are sitting in, the breath you are breathing, the eyes you see with, the balance to walk, the ability to exercise, the brain cells to think, the insides to digest food, and the taste buds to enjoy it (He didn't have to do that, you know). How many thousands of ways are we dependent on the Lord every day? Sadly, like oblivious children, we fail to thank Him nearly as often as we should. Perhaps this is one of the reasons why in the dreadful picture of life outside of God in Romans 1, Paul says that He pours out wrath on those who "did not glorify Him as God or show gratitude" (Rom. 1:21).

So join me. Join me in repenting of our toddler-like ignoring of the countless ways our Father has taken care of us. Give thanks. He spares nothing for us, even his own Son. Join me in cultivating a heart brimming with gratitude.

The author who has most helped me with gratitude is N.D. Wilson. In his recent book, *Death By Living*, he writes:

> As the earth screams through space, balanced exactly on the edge of everyone burning alive and everyone freezing solid, as we shriek through deadly obstacle courses of meteor showers and find them picturesque, as the nearest fiery star vomits eruptions hundreds of times bigger that (*sic*) our wee planet (giving chipper local weathermen northern lights to chatter about), as a giant reflective rock glides around us slopping the seas (and never falls down), and as we ride in our machines, darting past fools and drunks and texting teenagers, how many times do we thank God? We are always in His hands, but we often feel like we are in our own. We can't thank Him for every breath and every heartbeat, but we can thank Him every day for not splatting us with the moon or letting us drop into the sun. When a drunk crushes some family, some mother, some friend; when a story ends, then we wake up. Then we turn to God with confused expressions, wanting to know why He was sleeping in the boat. He

brought us here from nothing; is He ever allowed to take us to an exit? His own Son died young; do you think He doesn't understand? Moses didn't see the Promised Land. Samson died blind in the rubble. Stephen beneath stones. Paul without a head. Peter upside down. In a bed or on the battlefield or on asphalt in shattered glass beneath a flashing light, we are God's stories to end. How many drunks has He spared you from? Thank Him before you ask to be spared from another. How many breaths have you drawn? How many winter winds have tightened your skin? How many Christmases have you seen? How many times has the sky swirled glory above your head like a benediction? See it. Hear Him. Thank Him. Ask for more. Search for moments in your story for which you can be grateful....Gratitude is liberation. We are all mortals, called into this narrative in this timestream without our consent. And we will all reach an end. See the gifts. And if they seem sparse, start counting. Omit nothing. Can you count that high? You may have less than others do, like the widow with two small coins in the temple. God had given her little, but what did she do with her little?[8]

For what does Paul thank God?

Their gifts to his ministry. In many ways, *Philippians* is a missionary support letter. Paul writes to update them on his personal circumstances, to report on how the gospel is spreading, to offer spiritual encouragement, and to express gratitude for the many ways they have reinforced his mission.

He describes it as a "partnership in the gospel" (1:5). The word for partnership (*koinōnia*) is often used of financial cooperation.[9] For example, toward the end of Romans, Paul writes, "Macedonia and Achaia were pleased to make a contribution (*koinōnia*) for the poor among the saints in Jerusalem" (Rom. 15:26).[10] He thanks God for their money given for the spread of the gospel.

He is also thankful because he knows that God will finish what He started in the Philippians (1:6). *God* is the one who initiates good works. Even faith is from Him (1:29). And what He begins He also sustains until Christ returns. There may be bumps along the way, but He *will* bring it to completion.

Why, though, is Paul so confident? Because of the fruit he has seen in their lives (Phil. 1:7). They are partners with him *in grace*.[11] They pray for the mission of God. They give generously to it. They take care of his temporal needs while in prison.[12] In every way, they are truly co-laborers in Paul's gospel ministry, which earned his confidence that their faith was real. Would he have the same confidence in us? As we saw above, true conversion inevitably and necessarily leads to a desire to see others converted.

When does Paul pray?

Always? Yes, always. Elsewhere he says, "Pray constantly" (1 Thes. 5:17). We need to broaden our understanding of prayer. We do need special times set apart for prayer, but we also need to make the most of the minutia of everyday life. We need to redeem our down time, our commutes, our work, our cleaning. We need to transform every moment of every day into fellowship with God.

In the Old Covenant, before Jesus came, there was a certain time and place for offerings: scheduled sacrifices made at the temple. In the New Covenant, we offer our whole beings as living sacrifices (Rom. 12:1-2). There is no longer an altar – all of life is worship. One NT scholar writes, "If 'the holy place' is where sacrifice is to be offered, precisely in its set-apartness from the commonplace of everyday usage, Paul in effect transforms the holy place into the marketplace. He 'secularizes' the sanctuary by sanctifying the business of every day."[13] Worship is not just a Sunday morning activity, it's a life activity. We too easily compartmentalize our everyday and ordinary existence from our spirituality. In the words of Brother Lawrence, we need to develop the "holy habit" of communing with God throughout the day, praying always. We are already talking to ourselves; we might as well make the chatter useful by directing it toward God. Embrace a full-time surrendered awareness of Him in the present moment. Take every thought captive to the obedience of Christ (2 Cor. 10:5).

Notes

1. Tom Wright, *Paul for Everyone: The Prison Letters* (Louisville, KY: Westminster John Knox Press, 2004), 83.

2. Jerry L. Sumney, *Philippians: A Greek Student's Intermediate Reader* (Peabody, MA: 10 Hendrickson, 2007), 3.

3. Murray J. Harris, *Slave of Christ: A New Testament Metaphor for Total Devotion to Christ* (Downers Grove, IL: InterVarsity Press, 1999), 18.

4. Karl Barth, *Epistle to the Philippians* (Louisville, KY: Westminster John Knox, 2002), 10; See David Peterson, *Possessed by God: A New Testament Theology of Sanctification and Holiness* (Downers Grove, IL: InterVarsity, 1995).

5. The office of overseer is the same office as pastor or elder.

6. Cf. Acts 20:28, Titus 1:5-7, 1 Pet. 5:1-2.

7. Paul was so grace-*full* that he changed the normal Greek greeting *chairein* (greetings) to *charis* (grace). Sumney, *Philippians*, 5.

8. N.D. Wilson, *Death By Living* (Nashville, TN: Thomas Nelson, 2013), 139-40, 110.

9. Sumney, *Philippians*, 9, 13; Carson, *Basics*, 16; Hooker, *The Letter to the Philippians*, 483. Wright, *Paul for Everyone*, 84.

10. Cf. Rom. 12:13, 2 Cor. 9:13, Gal. 6:6.

11. I love the way the Holy Spirit describes it. He doesn't say partners in mission, partners in labor, partners in the faith, or partners in suffering. He could have, but He calls them partners in grace. God's Riches At Christ's Expense.

12. Roman prisons were not rehabilitative. Friends were vital to provide life's necessities and to make it bearable.

13. James D.G. Dunn, *The Theology of Paul the Apostle* (Grand Rapids, MI: Eerdmans, 1998), 544. The reader should note I have several *major* disagreements with several aspects of Dunn's work.

3

Praying God's Way

Who should pray more? *All hands go up.*

Robert Murray M'Cheyne writes, "What a man is alone on his knees before God, that he is, and no more."[1] Similarly, J.I. Packer says, "I believe that prayer is the measure of the man, spiritually, in a way that nothing else is, so that how we pray is as important a question as we can ever face."[2]

It is easy to make people feel guilty about their lack of prayer, but rather than being reminded of how terrible we are, I think we need inspiration. Philippians 1:8-11 gives us just that:

> *For God is my witness, how I deeply miss all of you with the affection of Christ Jesus. And I pray this: that your love will keep on growing in knowledge and every kind of discernment, so that you can determine what really matters and can be pure and blameless in the day of Christ, filled with the fruit of righteousness that comes through Jesus Christ, to the glory and praise of God.*

We can glean four things from this God-centered prayer:

First, **we should pray for one another.** Paul prayed for all the Philippians (1:4), asking God to make their love abound more and more. While we should pray for those outside our church family, those inside should be our first priority.

Second, **we should pray with affection.** Paul missed this church deeply. We should long for our fellow church members. You say, *I really don't care that much for anyone in my church family.* Well, the honesty is appreciated, but you need to work on that. The fastest road to affection is the one paved with action. When we act for the good of another, that is to say when we *love* them, more often than not our hearts follow. C.S. Lewis writes,

> The rule for all of us is perfectly simple. Do not waste time bothering whether you "love" your neighbor; act as if you did. As soon as we do this we find one of the great secrets. When you are behaving as if you loved someone, you will presently come to love him.[3]

Notice it is the *affection of Christ Jesus.* This shows us two things. First, and amazingly, Jesus has affection for us. He longs for us. Oh, how He loves us. We are His portion, and He is our prize. As the hymn goes:

> *The church's one foundation is Jesus Christ her Lord*
> *She is his new creation by water and the Word*
> *From heaven he came and sought her to be his holy bride*
> *With his own blood he bought her, and for her life he died*

And second, affection for one another comes through Jesus. There are many people in our congregations who are very different from us, but because we are one with Jesus, we are one with each other. That opens the door for deep affection.

Third, **we should pray for love to grow.** Is this love for God or love for one another? Paul probably leaves it vague and ambiguous because the two are tied together.[4] Vertical love and horizontal love are inextricably bound: "If anyone says, 'I love God,' yet hates his brother, he is a liar. For the person who does not love his brother he has seen cannot love the God he has not seen. And we have this command from Him: The one who loves God must also love his brother. Everyone who believes that Jesus is the Messiah has been born of God, and everyone who loves the Father also loves the one born of Him" (1 John 4:20-5:1). Love for God demands love for one another. Both must increase.

Having said that, Paul is probably primarily concerned about their love for one another. In Philippians 2:2, he exhorts them to "have the same love." In 1 Thessalonians 3:12, he prays that they would "increase and overflow with love for one another and for everyone." In Ephesians 3:17, he prays for the church to be "rooted and firmly established in love." He probably has the same kind of thing in mind here.

He prays that their love will grow *in knowledge and every kind of discernment*. That isn't about knowledge, in general. The Holy Spirit is not concerned about physics, biology, or math, but knowledge of God's Word and God's ways.[5] This is similar to Colossians 1:9-10:

> *For this reason also, since the day we heard this, we haven't stopped praying for you. We are asking that you may be filled with the knowledge of His will in all wisdom and spiritual understanding, so that you may walk worthy of the Lord, fully pleasing to Him, bearing fruit in every good work and growing in the knowledge of God" (cf. Eph. 1:17).*

How do we grow in this knowledge? It definitely does not happen on its own. First and foremost, it comes through Bible reading. It also comes through faithful attendance to worship services, Sunday school, home groups, and other avenues your church provides for teaching and discussion of the Word of God. It also happens through exposure to Christian truth. Do you value reading solid Christian books that help you grasp the message of Scripture? What is the ratio of time spent reading Scripture or Christian books in comparison to watching the TV? We have a fridge magnet with a picture of a television on it that reads, "Think outside the box; read a book."[6]

You will find that growing in the knowledge of God is fuel for the fire of worship. And it never runs out. The more we love, the more we learn, and the more we learn, the more we love. This is why Paul prays in Ephesians that we may be able to comprehend the length, and width, and height, and depth of God's love and to "know the Messiah's love that surpasses knowledge" (Eph. 3:19). We must strive after and pray for the knowledge that is unknowable – the love of Jesus.

Fourth, we should pray so that we "can approve the things that are superior." Growing in love means being able to determine what really matters. There are lots of gray areas in the Christian life, and we need Spirit-produced discernment to determine what is best. We need sanctified common sense in the New Covenant. Romans 12:2 famously reads, "Do not be conformed to this age, but be transformed by the renewing of your mind, so that you may discern what is the good, pleasing, and perfect will of God." There is a freedom in the New Covenant that was lacking under the Law. You would never hear a good Jew talk of discerning the will of God apart from Torah, but this is exactly what the apostle is praying we'll do. We need to approve the superior things so that we will be ready for the day of Christ. Martin Luther said there were two days on his calendar: this and that. All we do has *that* day in mind.

Becoming loving, pure, and blameless is a lifelong affair. The process is slow, sometimes painfully so, but we are progressing. "We are not yet what we ought to be. But by the grace of God we are not what we were."[7] Jesus said that the pure are blessed because they will see God (Matt. 5:8). Are you striving after purity of heart? Is there any known sin in your life?

Our growth in purity can increase because we are filled with the righteousness that comes through Jesus Christ. This righteousness refers to our standing before God. We are sinners; God is holy. We are unrighteous; He is righteous. That's a problem because none of us can attain a right standing by our own good works. God must provide it. And He does, through Jesus. *Nothing in my hand I bring; simply to the cross I cling.*

Philippians 3:9 is a hugely important passage in this regard. Paul wants to "gain Christ and be found in Him, not having a righteousness of my own from the law, but one that is through faith in Christ – the righteousness from God based on faith." This is an alien righteousness. It is a gift from God. *My hope is built on nothing less than Jesus' blood and righteousness; I dare not trust the sweetest frame, but wholly lean on Jesus' name.* If you have believed the gospel, you have been filled with the fruit that comes from that right standing. Notice the order: the fruit (life transformation) comes *from* being declared "in the right" through faith. As good ole traditional Protestant theology has taught for 400 years, justification is the basis from which sanctification flows. Or as Tim Keller puts it, "Religion operates on the principle of 'I obey – therefore I am accepted by God.' The basic operating principle of the gospel is 'I am accepted by God through the work of Jesus Christ – therefore I obey.'"[8] And in good form, Paul notes that it is all for God's glory and praise. *Soli Deo Gloria.*

Do we pray this way? Sadly, usually we do not. We tend to focus on physical needs. We pray about jobs, sickness, cancer, children, comfort, and travel. And, praise God, He does care about such things. My mom always says if you can't take a pimple to God, you can't take a tumor. We can confidently cast all our cares on Him because He cares for us (1 Pet. 5:7), but our greatest cares ought to go beyond the temporal and mundane. We should pray mostly for eternal things, gospel things, and love.

A good prayer life takes devotion and work. First and foremost, we must plan to pray. John Piper writes,

> Unless I'm badly mistaken, one of the main reasons so many of God's children don't have a significant life of prayer is not so much that we don't want to, but that we don't plan to. If you want to take a four-week vacation, you don't just get up one summer morning and say, 'Hey, let's go today!' You won't have anything ready. You won't know where to go. Nothing has been planned. But that is how many of us treat prayer. We get up day after day and realize that significant times of prayer should be a part of our life, but nothing's ever ready. We don't know where to go. Nothing has been planned. No time. No place. No procedure. And we all know that the opposite of planning is not a wonderful flow of deep, spontaneous experiences in prayer. The opposite of planning is the rut. If you don't plan a vacation, you will probably stay at home and watch TV. The natural, unplanned flow of spiritual life sinks to the lowest ebb of vitality. There is a race to be run and a fight to be fought. If you want renewal in your life of prayer, you must plan to see it.

Therefore, my simple exhortation is this: Let us take

time this very day to rethink our priorities and how prayer fits in. Make some new resolve. Try some new venture with God. Set a time. Set a place. Choose a portion of Scripture to guide you. Don't be tyrannized by the press of busy days. We all need midcourse corrections. Make this a day of turning to prayer – for the glory of God and for the fullness of your joy.[9]

Brothers and sisters, let's plan to pray.

Notes

1. Quoted in D.A. Carson, *A Call to Spiritual Reformation* (Grand Rapids, MI: Baker), 16.

2. J.I. Packer in *My Path of Prayer*, ed. David Hanes (Worthing, West Sussex: Henry E. Walter, 1981), 56.

3. C.S. Lewis, *Mere Christianity*, 110 in *The Complete C.S. Lewis* (New York, NY: HarperOne, 2002).

4. Carson, *Basics for Believers*, 20.

5. Carson, *Basics for Believers*, 20.

6. While I am not opposed to all TV, many of us probably need to heed the famous words of Neil Postman: "This is one use of television – as a source of illuminating the printed page." *Amusing Ourselves to Death* (New York, NY: Penguin, 1985), 83.

7. Carson, *A Call to Spiritual Reformation*, 135.

8. Tim Keller, *Prodigal God* (New York, NY: Dutton, 2008), 114.

9. John Piper, *Desiring God* (Sisters, OR: Multnomah, 2003), 182-83.

[4]

Trials and the Kingdom of Christ

Now I want you to know, brothers, that what has happened to me has actually resulted in the advance of the gospel, so that it has become known throughout the whole imperial guard, and to everyone else, that my imprisonment is in the cause of Christ. Most of the brothers in the Lord have gained confidence from my imprisonment and dare even more to speak the message fear-lessly. To be sure, some preach Christ out of envy and strife, but others out of good will. These do so out of love, knowing that I am appointed for the defense of the gospel; the others proclaim Christ out of rivalry, not sincerely, seeking to cause me anxiety in my imprisonment. What does it matter? Just that in every way, whether out of false motives or true, Christ is proclaimed. And in this I rejoice. Yes, and I will rejoice because I know this will lead to my deliverance through your prayers and help from the Spirit of Jesus Christ. (Philippians 1:12-19)

Trials

Being in Christ doesn't necessarily keep one from being in chains.[1] Contrary to what many TV preachers teach, trials do not mean that you lack faith or are missing God's will. Acts 14:22 says, "It is necessary to pass through many troubles on our way into the kingdom of God." Jesus said, "You will have suffering in this world. Be courageous! I have conquered the world" (John

16:33). Difficult times are to be expected for Christians, but God uses them for kingdom purposes.

Paul's imprisonment may have seemed like a hindrance. Here we have a traveling apostle who can no longer travel, which is like a chef with no taste buds, or a concert pianist having her hands tied behind her back.[2] But even when Paul can no longer be on mission, God can. The gospel spreads even through the most unlikely circumstances. He established His Kingdom through the execution of the King!

Are you facing trials right now? If not, you will be soon enough. Don't be discouraged. Follow Paul's example as he views his situation with Christ-centered lenses. He knows that God is in control and that God is good. That is why when he was arrested, he sang hymns rather than issuing complaints (Acts 16). When you know deep down in your bones that God is sovereign and that He can be trusted, it gives you a steel backbone. Come what may, this is God's world, and He knows what He is doing. He has good purposes for His children. Romans 8:28 never gets old: "We know that all things work together for the good of those who love God: those who are called according to His purpose." Take courage!

Throughout history, God has used persecution to grow the Church. In AD 197, Tertullian said, "The blood of the martyrs is the seed of the church." When non-Christians observe how Christians suffer, they are compelled to know more about the God we serve. They will ask about our hope (1 Pet. 3:14-15). The blood and pain of the saints is the fertilizer for the multiplication of Abraham's seed.

Like the indigenous missionary who walked barefoot from village to village preaching the gospel in India: One day after a very long trip and much discouragement, he entered a village, but was spurned and rejected. Exhausted, he went to the edge of the village and lay down under a tree to get some rest. When he awoke, the whole town was gathered around to hear him. They had come to check him out, and when they saw his blistered feet they concluded that he must be a holy man. They felt bad for rejecting him and wanted to hear his message.[3]

Or Natasha, whose story is told in Sergei Kourdakov's auto-biography. Kourdakov was commissioned by the Russian secret police to raid Christian prayer gatherings and persecute believers with extraordinary brutality and violence. The afflictions of one believer changed his life:

> I saw Victor Matveyev reach and grab for a young girl [Natasha Zhdanova] who was trying to escape to another room. She was a beautiful young girl. *What a waste to be a Believer.* Victor caught her, picked her above his head, and held her high in the air for a second. She was pleading, "Don't, please don't. Dear God, help us!" Victor threw her so hard she hit the wall at the same height she was thrown, then dropped to the floor, semiconscious, moaning. Victor turned and laughed and exclaimed, "I'll bet the idea of God went flying out of her head."

On a later raid, Sergei was shocked to see Natasha again.

> I quickly surveyed the room and saw a sight I couldn't believe. There she was, the same girl! It couldn't be. But it was. Only three nights before, she had been at the other meeting and had been viciously thrown across the room. It was the first time I really got a good look at her. She was more beautiful than I had first remembered—a very beautiful girl with long, flowing blond hair, large blue eyes, and smooth skin, one of the most naturally beautiful girls I have ever seen....
>
> I picked her up and flung her on a table facedown. Two of us stripped her clothes off. One of my men held her down and I began to beat her again and again. My hands began to sting under the blows. Her skin started to blister. I continued to beat her, until pieces of bloody flesh came off on my hand. She moaned but fought desperately not to cry. To suppress her cries, she bit her lower lip until it was bitten through and blood ran down her chin.
>
> At last she gave in and began sobbing. When I was so exhausted I couldn't raise my arm for even one more blow, and her backside was a mass of raw flesh, I pushed her off the table, and she collapsed on the floor.

To Sergei's shock, he later encountered her at yet *another* prayer meeting, but this time something was different:

There *she* was again—Natasha Zhdanova!

Several of the guys saw her too. Alex Gulyaev moved toward Natasha, hatred filling his face, his club raised above his head.

Then something I never expected to see suddenly happened. Without warning, Victor jumped between Natasha and Alex, facing Alex head-on.

"Get out of my way," Alex shouted angrily.

Victor's feet didn't move. He raised his club and said menacingly, "Alex, I'm telling you, don't touch her! No one touches her!"

I listened in amazement. Incredibly, one of my most brutal men was protecting one of the Believers! "Get back!" he shouted to Alex. "Get back or I'll let you have it." He shielded Natasha, who was cowering on the floor.

Angered, Alex shouted, "You want her for yourself, don't you?"

"No," Victor shouted back. "She has something we don't have! Nobody touches her! Nobody!"

...For one of the first times in my life, I was deeply moved...Natasha *did* have something! She had been beaten horribly. She had been warned and threatened. She had gone through unbelievable suffering, but here she was again. Even Victor had been moved and recognized it. She had something we didn't have. I wanted to run after her and ask, "What is it?" I wanted to talk to her, but she was gone. This heroic Christian girl who had suffered so much at our hands somehow touched and troubled me very much.

The Lord later opened Sergei's heart to the glorious good news of Jesus Christ. As he reflected on Natasha, whom he never saw again, he wrote:

"And, finally, to Natasha, whom I beat terribly and who was willing to be beaten a third time for her faith, I want to say, Natasha, largely because of you, my life is now changed and I am a fellow Believer in Christ with you. I have a new life before me. God has forgiven me; I hope you can also.

Thank you, Natasha, wherever you are.

I will never, never forget you."[4]

When Christians lose a job, we don't panic. When a loved one dies, we don't grieve hopelessly. When we get sick, we don't despair but entrust ourselves to the One who cares for us. When wronged, we do not revile in return. When persecuted, we do not curse, we bless. This kind of perseverance provokes questions.

Bold Evangelism

Paul admits that preaching Christ can be a fearful thing (1:14). This encourages me because I often fear the opinion of others when evangelizing. Isn't that the main reason most of us do not witness more? Natasha makes us all look like a bunch of faithless cowards, which is why we need to be reminded of such stories.

How do we get over this fear? Here are six ways –

First, fear God: "Therefore, because we know the fear of the Lord, we seek to persuade people" (2 Cor. 5:11). When you see God for who He is, and grasp the reality of sin, grace, and judgment, the opinions of people become small. *Second*, grasp the gospel: "For Christ's love compels us, since we have reached this conclusion: If One died for all, then all died" (2 Cor. 5:14). *Third*, love people. The most loving thing we can do for someone is tell them about Jesus. Eternity is at stake. *Fourth*, trust the message. The gospel is the power of God for salvation (Rom. 1:16). The gospel *works* – God saves through it (Col. 1:6). *Fifth*, do it. Speak the message, and you will find that though you may be dreadfully slouching on the way to tell someone about Jesus, you will be joyfully skipping on the return. *Finally*, surround yourself with faithful and mature Christian friends. Read Christian biographies, especially of missionaries. Their faithfulness will embolden you.

Only That Christ Is Proclaimed

Some people preach Christ with wrong motives (1:15-17). They are envious, contentious, and insincere, evangelizing out of rivalry, the very thing God commands us to avoid in the next chapter (Phil. 2:3; cf. 2:21). They really care about themselves, not the lost. But the message is what matters (1:18-19).[5] As long as it is preached, even if by pretentious preachers, Paul will rejoice.

It is important to realize, though, that Paul is not affirming a false message about Jesus. One only needs to keep reading Philippians to see this. In 3:2, he warns of those who distort the gospel by adding to it, calling them dogs and evil workers. In 2 Corinthians 11:3-4, he chastises the Corinthians, saying, "But I fear that, as the serpent deceived Eve by his cunning, your minds may be seduced from a complete and pure devotion to Christ. For if a person comes and preaches another Jesus, whom we did not preach, or you receive a different spirit, which you had not received, or a different gospel, which you had not accepted, you put up with it splendidly!" Similarly, in Galatians he says that even if the false gospel is taught by an apostle or an angel, then damn the apostle and the angel to Hell (Gal. 1:8-9). Paul certainly does not rejoice when "another" Christ is preached, but if the message is pure and undiluted, he doesn't care about the speaker's motive or his own reputation. All that matters is the advancement of the gospel.[6]

Petty opinions fall to the wayside when Christ is central. Black carpet, blue carpet, or green carpet? *Christ is proclaimed!* Pews or movie seats? *Christ is proclaimed!* Methodist, Presbyterian, or Baptist? *Christ is proclaimed!* Contemporary music or traditional music? *Christ is proclaimed!* Friends, let us always keep the main thing the main thing, and when it is, *rejoice!*

Notes

1. Fowl, *Philippians*, 39.

2. Wright, *Paul for Everyone: The Prison Letters*, 89.

3. Recounted in John Piper, *Let the Nations be Glad!* (Grand Rapids, MI: Baker Books, 1993), 94-95.

4. Quoted in John Piper, *Desiring God* (Sisters, OR: Multnomah, 2003), 275-78.

5. Note the emphasis on "gospel," "Christ," "Lord," "message" in this small section.

6. "I know this will lead to my deliverance" is straight from Job 13:16, showing that Paul sees himself as a righteous sufferer who trusts God.

Making Much of Jesus

My eager expectation and hope is that I will not be ashamed about anything, but that now as always, with all boldness, Christ will be highly honored in my body, whether by life or by death. For me, living is Christ and dying is gain. Now if I live on in the flesh, this means fruitful work for me; and I don't know which one I should choose. I am pressured by both. I have the desire to depart and be with Christ – which is far better – but to remain in the flesh is more necessary for you. Since I am persuaded of this, I know that I will remain and continue with all of you for your progress and joy in the faith, so that, because of me, your confidence may grow in Christ Jesus when I come to you again. (Philippians 1:20-26)

The Meaning of Your Life

What is the over-arching purpose of your life? The right answer is – to highly honor Jesus Christ. Paul makes that point when he says, "My eager expectation and hope is that I will not be ashamed about anything, but that now as always, with all bold-ness, Christ will be highly honored in my body, whether by life or by death." His aim is to make much of Jesus. He wants to show Jesus' greatness. He wants Jesus to be magnified. Exalted.

This is no mere wish but a hopeful expectation because he plans to live that way with *all boldness*. We shouldn't cower at the thought of ridicule but should represent the King with confidence precisely because He is the King. God wants believers to speak of Christ without fear, to be unashamed in representing Him, and to increase our joy in the faith.

We should make it our aim to make much of Jesus in every circumstance, "whether by life or by death." Are we this Christ-obsessed? Is He central in our hearts and lives? Every moment of every day presents us with an opportunity to be ashamed of Christ or to make much of Him. Annie Dillard once said, "How we spend our days is, of course, how we spend our lives." Lives spent exalting Christ consist of days spent exalting Christ, and days spent exalting Christ consist of a hundred small, everyday moments in which we seek to live for King Jesus.

Christian, Christ is your life. Your number one priority is no longer you, but Him (2 Cor. 5:15). You exist for Christ and for Christ-centered ministry.[1] Paul gave his life to expand, to build up, and to encourage the body of Christ. This is what your life is for too! Paul was not concerned with personal interests. It would have been better for him to be done with the suffering of this life and to go live with His Savior, but it was better for the church if he lived a while longer. He lived the principle of cruciform love, of dying to self for the good of others, what might be called the *Jesus mindset* of chapter two: "Do nothing out of rivalry or conceit, but in humility consider others as more important than yourselves. Everyone should look out not only for his own interests, but also for the interests of others. Make your own attitude that of Christ Jesus, who, existing in the form of God, did not consider equality with God as something to be used for His own advantage. Instead He emptied Himself by assuming the form of a slave, taking on the likeness of men. And when He had come as a man in His external form, He humbled Himself by becoming obedient to the point of death – even to death on a cross." Your life is not about fulfilling your desires, but Christ's desires.

The Benefit of Dying

How can Paul say, "To die is gain"? This is the opposite of the way the world views death. People try to deal with the fear of death by denying it. Just look at the cosmetic surgery industry, and our refusal to admit that we are outwardly wasting away. Look at the millions of dollars people spend during the last weeks of their life. Every gray hair (or lost hair) and wrinkle is an indictment. Have you ever noticed how our culture is fascinated with youth? How often do you see elderly people holding microphones? Almost never. We have a youth fetish. Sadly, evangelical churches have largely followed our culture which finds elderly people disturbing and annoying. This is because age and deterioration remind us that death is coming. The wages of sin is death. Woody Allen said that he doesn't fear death, he just doesn't want to be there when it happens. Louis XV demanded that those around him not even use the word *death*. Guess what! He died anyway. Try as they might to deny it, graveyards continue to fill up. You will die. I will die. Death is God's punishment for sin, starting with our first parents. But God sent His one and only Son so that if we will trust in Him, death will not have the final word – we will rise to live with Him forever.

Do you view death as gain? It is okay to dread death (see Phil. 2:27), but that is not the same as fearing. Christians have no reason to fear death. Why would we? Hebrews 2:14-15 says that Jesus shared in our humanity "so that through His death He might destroy the one holding the power of death – that is, the Devil – and free those who were held in slavery all their lives by the fear of death." Our greatest treasure lies on the other side of death. It is Jesus Himself.[2] Ligon Duncan writes,

> On the one hand, death is the last enemy. Believers, too, are sinners, and so unless the Lord comes soon, we will all taste death. The Christian views death as an enemy; it is not a natural part of life. Death is actually the way things were never intended to be. Death is a judgment of God against sin. Death is the most unnatural thing in this world. But on the other hand, death has become for the believer an entrance into glory."[3]

Death has lost its sting. Death has been defeated and destroyed through the death of Jesus. We need not fear it. How freeing! The evangelist D.L. Moody once remarked, "Some day you will read in the papers that D.L. Moody, of East Northfield, is dead. Don't you believe a word of it! At that moment I shall be more alive than I am now."[4]

If the thought of being with your Lord does not excite you, I am not sure why you claim to be a Christian. Our greatest desire should be to be with Jesus. Incidentally, our main desire for Heaven should not be to reunite with family. I recall attending a youth evangelistic event called *Heaven's Gates, Hell's Flames*. True to their Finneyistic theology, their method was to manipulate emotions and to literally "scare the Hell" out of kids. One scene portrayed the death of a young girl in a car accident. Her parents had died years before. As the little girl entered Heaven's gates, she ran right past Jesus (the door man!) and into the arms of her parents. Then came the appeal: "You want to see your family again after death, don't you? Pray this prayer, sign this card, and you will." Obviously, this is a distorted perspective. Yes, in God's kindness, we will see departed loved ones who are in Christ, but our primary desire ought to be Jesus.

In these verses, we learn a bit about what happens during what is commonly called the "intermediate state," the period between our death and Christ's return. At death, believers are ushered into the presence of the Lord (1:23; cf. 2 Cor. 5:8). We see this when Jesus assured the thief on the cross that he would be in paradise that very day (Luke 23:43). This "going to be with the Lord" is what we mean by *Heaven*.[5] Heaven will be glorious, but it's not our final resting place.[6] Later in Philippians, Paul writes, "He will transform the body of our humble condition into the likeness of His glorious body, by the power that enables Him to subject everything to Himself" (3:21, cf. Phil. 3:11). Our bodies will come back to life and live on a renovated earth. This is why the Bible calls death "sleep," which implies that we will "wake up" (1 Cor. 15:51-52, 1 Thess. 4:14). We die to go to the Lord, soul ripped asunder from body, but when Christ returns they will be reunited in resurrection life.[7]

Because of that future hope, life here and now must be about making much of Jesus, whether by life or by death. Paul was sold out to the Lord in this way. For him, life meant ministry, death was gain, and suffering made him more like Jesus and advanced the gospel. What can the world or Satan do to a man or woman of God who views life like that?[8]

John Chrysostom, the famous monk turned priest who was born in 349, writes, "If the empress wishes to banish me, let her do so; 'the earth is the Lord's.' If she wants to have me sawn asunder, I will have Isaiah for an example. If she wants me to be drowned in the ocean, I think of Jonah. If I am to be thrown in the fire, the three men in the furnace suffered the same. If cast before wild beasts, I remember Daniel in the lion's den. If she wants me to be stoned, I have before me Stephen, the first martyr. If she demands my head, let her do so; John the Baptist shines before me. Naked I came from my mother's womb, naked shall I leave this world. Paul reminds me, 'If I still pleased men, I would not be the servant of Christ.'"[9]

This is why you were created. This is what you are here for. This should be the over-arching purpose of your life. To make Jesus look great! All the time. With all boldness. In life or death.

Notes

1. Fowl, *Philippians*, 49; Carson, *Basics for Believers*, 29.

2. Paul uses this same word "gain" (*kerdos*) in the next chapter. What *was* gain to him is now loss because of Jesus (Phil. 3:7). So death is gain because we have already counted all but Christ as loss. In death, we gain Christ in a fresh way.

3. Ligon Duncan, *Fear Not!* (Scotland: Christian Focus, 2001), 17.

4. William R. Moody, *The Life of Dwight L. Moody* (Grand Rapids, MI: Revell, 1900), iii quoted in Chandler, *To Live is Christ*, 38.

5. I hasten to add there is not a single syllable in all of Scripture to undergird the idea of purgatory. Rather, my sin, not in part but *the whole*, has been nailed to the cross, and I bear it no more. Praise the Lord, O my soul!

6. I own a great little book entitled, *Heaven...It's Not the End of the World* by David Lawrence.

7. N.T. Wright: "The ultimate destination is (once more) not 'going to heaven when you die' but being bodily raised into the transformed, glorious likeness of Jesus Christ." *Surprised by Hope* (New York, NY: HarperOne, 2008), 168.

8. Chandler, *To Live is Christ*, 24-25.

9. Saint Chrysostom, *Saint Chrysostom on the Priesthood Ascetic Treatises, Select Homilies and Letters and Homilies on the Statutes*, ed. Philip Schaff (Whitefish, MT: Kessinger Publishing, 2004), 14 quoted in Chandler, *To Live is Christ*, 24-25.

6

Living Worthy of the Gospel

Just one thing: Live your life in a manner worthy of the gospel of Christ. Then, whether I come and see you or am absent, I will hear about you that you are standing firm in one spirit, with one mind, working side by side for the faith that comes from the gospel, not being frightened in any way by your opponents. This is a sign of destruction for them, but of your deliverance – and this is from God. For it has been given to you on Christ's behalf not only to believe in Him, but also to suffer for Him, having the same struggle that you saw I had and now hear that I have. (Philippians 1:27-30)

"Just one thing...," these sorts of God-breathed comments ought to get our attention. "Just one thing: live your life in a manner worthy of the gospel." Paul is speaking in *civil* terms here. He means "to live as a worthy citizen." One NT scholar translates this phrase as "Live out your citizenship in a manner worthy of the gospel of Christ."[1] Since Philippi was a Roman colony, his readers would have understood the privileges and obligations of Roman citizenship and how Paul compared that to the Christian life. God is concerned that we are good citizens – not of Philippi or America – but of the gospel. Or, as he puts it in 3:20, "our citizenship is in Heaven." We are called to have *heavenly* values, to be loyal to *Messiah's* empire, and to be consumed with the success of *His* Kingdom.

A person living worthy of the gospel will walk in unity with fellow believers. He or she will be "firm in one spirit, with one mind, working side by side." Paul exhorts the same in the next chapter: "Fulfill my joy by thinking the same way, having the same love, sharing the same feelings, focusing on one goal" (2:2). This "same mind" is the mind of Christ (2:5 NIV). With Him as the basis of our unity, we will work together for His honor.

A person living worthy of the gospel will also work for the faith that comes from the gospel (Phil. 1:27). To be a Christian is to be active. For this reason, we ought to reconsider the language we often use in local churches. For example, the term "membership" wreaks of passivity. The local church is not a country club. I prefer the "partnership" language we have seen in Philippians. The Philippians are partners in the gospel (Phil. 1:5) and of grace (Phil. 1:7). That is our model.

Division often comes because we are no longer working for the gospel but for our own agendas. When we major on the minors, gospel advancement ceases or at least slows. Thom Rainer, CEO of *Lifeway*, said, "When the 'preferences' of the church members are greater than their 'passion for the gospel,' the church is dying." Paul majored on the majors: Christ is preached, and in this he rejoiced.

A person living worthy of the gospel will not fear people: "not being frightened in any way by your opponents. This is a sign of destruction for them, but of your deliverance – and this is from God" (1:28). We don't know a lot about these opponents, but we know that they were tempting the Philippians to be afraid to speak the message. But just as faith is God's gift,[2] so is suffering. Did you know that? Do you look at suffering as given by God? The word here literally means "graciously given" (*charizō-mai*). Suffering is not due to a failure to walk as a worthy citizen of the gospel but is a gracious gift that results from walking as a worthy citizen of the gospel.[3]

There are a lot of false teachers on TV who teach that Christians are supposed to be happy and healthy, and that the presence of suffering means the absence of God's blessing. But Paul says something else. Being in Christ does not keep one from being in chains. Christianity and affliction go together. We serve a *crucified* King, after all. The pattern of Christ is the pattern of the Christian life. For Him, it was suffering *then* glory (Phil. 2:9-11), and the same goes for us (Phil. 3:10-11).

The Scriptures present us with four powerful themes that are massively helpful resources when dealing with suffering.[4] First is the sovereignty of God. The famous Baptist preacher Charles Spurgeon once wrote, "It would be a very sharp and trying experience to me to think that I have an affliction which God never sent me, that the bitter cup was never filled by his hand, that my trials were never measured out by him, nor sent to me by his arrangement of their weight and quantity."[5] Often we will blame the devil or others for our pain and suffering, but ultimately they come from God.

Consider Job, who was a righteous man. His suffering was not a result of his sin, rather it was because of a discussion that took place in the angelic realm, a discussion that Job knew nothing about. The Lord had said to Satan, "Have you considered my servant Job?" (Job 1:8). Satan replied that Job was only faithful because God was blessing him. God granted Satan permission to test Job through suffering. Note two things about this: 1) Job was righteous, so in no way was this ordeal punishment for his sins, and 2) God was in control over it. When Job lost his children, his livestock, and his servants, he fell to the ground and worshipped saying, "Naked I came from my mother's womb, and naked I will leave this life. The Lord gives, and the Lord takes away. Praise the name of Yahweh" (Job 1:21). He received his tough lot as God's doing.

Or consider Paul, who was given a thorn in the flesh *by God* (2 Cor. 12:7-10). But the purpose was far from Satanic. It was so that Paul would not exalt himself, and so that power would be perfected in weakness, as we sing, "When through fiery trials thy pathways shall lie, my grace, all-sufficient, shall be thy supply; the flame shall not hurt thee; I only design thy dross to consume, and thy gold to refine." God uses suffering to bring us to a point to which we would not arrive otherwise. Fire refines. God is sovereign over trials. It has been graciously granted to you to suffer for His sake.

The second theme is the Fall in Genesis 3. There we learn that God created a world without sin, death, or suffering. Suffering was not part of God's original design. It is an alien intruder into

God's good world. But since humanity rejected God as ruler, now the whole creation is fallen. The original design has been broken. Pain is now part of our existence.

The third theme is final judgment and the renewal of all things. If there were no judge, injustice would be left unpunished. We would be left to despair or to take matters into our own hands. But knowing that God will make all things right allows us to entrust ourselves to Him.

Fourth, the fact that God Himself became human and died shows us that He has experienced the darkness. He is the sovereign God who suffers. As Tim Keller puts it, "God is sovereign over suffering and yet, in teaching unique to the Christian faith among the major religions, God also made himself vulnerable and subject to suffering. The other side of the sovereignty of God is the suffering of God himself."[6]

In a book called *One Thousand Gifts*, Ann Voskamp shares how she struggled with losing her sister as a toddler. Her struggle boiled down to whether or not she trusted God. She writes, "[God] gave us Jesus...If God didn't withhold from us His very own Son, will God *withhold* anything we need? If trust must be earned, hasn't God unequivocally earned our trust with the bark on the raw wounds, the thorns pressed into the brow, your name on the cracked lips? How will He not also graciously give us all things He deems best and right? He's already given us the incomprehensible."[7]

Paul was a worthy example of how to respond to these trials. Sing. Rejoice. Work. He did this because his greatest desire, even greater than his own comfort, was to please Jesus. Are we centering our lives on Him? Do we make it our aim to see Him highly exalted, whether by life or by death? Can we say, "To live is Christ and to die is gain?" We suffer on *Christ's* behalf. It has been granted to believe in *Him*, and to suffer for *Him*. A life that isn't focused on the ultimate reason for its existence is wasted: you exist for Him! It is all about Him.

Notes

1. Sprinkle, *Fight*, 154. Fowl opts for "order your common life." *Philippians,*

60. Hooker: "to exercise the rights and duties of citizens." *The Letter to the Philippians*, 496.

2. God is the one who began a good work in us (Phil. 1:6). The Almighty is always the initiator. Faith is always a gift. Ephesians 2:8-9: "For you are saved by grace through faith, and this is not from yourselves; it is God's gift - not from works, so that no one can boast." This is grace, friends! Oh how helpful this is for our prayer lives as well: "God, give them faith." "God, open their hearts to hear just like you did with Lydia, the first convert in Philippi!" "God, save!"

3. Fowl, *Philippians*, 70.

4. This section is heavily indebted to Timothy Keller, *Walking With God Through Pain and Suffering* (New York, NY: Dutton, 2013), 113-22, though he does not include sovereignty in this section of his wonderful book.

5. Charles Spurgeon, *Christian History*, Issue 29, Vol. 10, No. 1, 25.

6. Keller, *Walking With God Through Pain and Suffering*, 147.

7. Ann Voskamp, *One Thousand Gifts* (Grand Rapids, MI: Zondervan, 2010), 154-55 quoted in Keller, *Walking With God Through Pain and Suffering*, 122.

7

The Jesus Mindset

We now turn to the most important section of Philippians and doubtless one of the most important of the whole NT:[1]

> *If then there is any encouragement in Christ, if any consolation of love, if any fellowship with the Spirit, if any affection and mercy, fulfill my joy by thinking the same way, having the same love, sharing the same feelings, focusing on one goal. Do nothing out of rivalry or conceit, but in humility consider others as more important than yourselves. Everyone should look out not only for his own interests, but also for the interests of others. Make your own attitude that of Christ Jesus, who, existing in the form of God, did not consider equality with God as something to be used for His own advantage. Instead He emptied Himself by assuming the form of a slave, taking on the likeness of men. And when He had come as a man in His external form, He humbled Himself by becoming obedient to the point of death – even to death on a cross. (Philippians 2:1-8)*

The passage naturally breaks into two points: the exhortation and the example.

Exhortation

Before the call to action, Paul gives the basis for it: "If then there is any encouragement in Christ, if any consolation of love, if any fellowship with the Spirit, if any affection and mercy." In other words, if you are a Christian these things are true: there *is* encouragement in Christ, there *is* consolation of love, there *is* fellowship with the Spirit, there *is* affection and mercy for God's people. And because those things are true of you, you can: "Complete my joy by being of the same mind, having the same love, being in full accord and of one mind" (ESV).[2]

God cares about unity of mindset, love, and feelings. How is this to work since where two believers are gathered, three opinions are among them? Preferences abound in worship music, leadership style, doctrinal issues, personality, political issues, parenting, education, and on and on. Yet when our main passion is gospel advancement, when we are focused on working side by side for the faith that comes from the gospel, we will be unified. We will have unity, even in the midst of diverse opinions, if we "do nothing out of rivalry or vain conceit." In other words, if your main focus is not *you*. If you are looking to the interests of others rather than to your own.[3]

We could just call this unity *love*. Love does not insist on its own way (1 Cor. 13:5). Love seeks to encourage and build up others, to serve them. The entire law is fulfilled in one statement: Love your neighbor as yourself (Gal. 5:13). Love looks for the opportunity to bless, it flees self-fulfillment and pursues the benefit of others.

This love-mindset is obviously important to God because Paul uses the verb *phroneō* twice in Philippians 2:2 and in chapter four to address a conflict between a couple of members: "I urge Euodia and I urge Syntyche to agree (*to auto phronein*) in the Lord" (Phil. 4:2).[4] He also uses it three other times in the NT:[5]

- Romans 12:16 – "Be in agreement with one another (*auto...phronountes*). Do not be proud; instead, associate with the humble. Do not be wise in your own estimation."

- Romans 15:5 – "Now may the God who gives endurance and encouragement allow you to live in harmony (*auto phronein*) with one another, according to the command of Christ Jesus."

- 2 Corinthians 13:11 – "Become mature, be encouraged, be of the same mind (*auto phroneite*), be at peace."

This love-mindset leads to self-mortifying action, a necessary work because sin is inherently selfish. One of the most accurate portraits of the human heart came in the film *Finding Nemo* with the seagulls who had a one-word vocabulary: "Mine, mine, mine." Self-centeredness is the sin beneath every sin. Self-centeredness "was the *original* original sin. When the serpent tempted Adam and Eve, he did it ultimately with self-exaltation: 'You will be like God,' he said. And every moment we operate out of selfish ambition and conceit, every time we think of ourselves as better than others or look only to our interests, we are essentially saying, 'I am God.'"[6] Therefore, loving others is not natural for us this side of the Fall.

So how do we create this kind of unity in our Christian communities? In his classic work, *Life Together*, Dietrich Bonhoeffer lays out seven helpful tips. Christians should:

1. Hold their tongues, refusing to speak uncharitably about a Christian brother or sister.

2. Cultivate the humility that comes from understanding that they, like Paul, are the greatest of sinners and can only live in God's sight by his grace.

3. Listen "long and patiently" so that they will understand their fellow Christian's need.

4. Refuse to consider their time and calling so valuable that they cannot be interrupted to help with unexpected needs, no matter how small or menial.

5. Bear the burden of their brothers and sisters in the Lord, both by preserving their freedom and by forgiving their sinful abuse of that freedom.

6. Declare God's word to their fellow believers when they need to hear it.

7. Understand that Christian authority is characterized by service and does not call attention to the person who performs the service.[7]

If every believer practiced these things, the world would see a more unified, loving Church.

Example

Jesus is the ultimate model of a self-denying, others-centered attitude. He embodied the love-mindset, most profoundly at Calvary. As John put it, "This is how we have come to know love: He laid down His life for us. We should also lay down our lives for our brothers" (1 John 3:16). The cross is both the objective provision for our salvation and the subjective pattern for the Christian life. Notice just a few passages:

- Ephesians 5:25 – "Husbands, love your wives, *just as Christ loved the church and gave Himself for her.*"

- John 13:34 – "I give you a new command: Love one another. *Just as I have loved you*, you must also love one another."

- 1 John 4:10 – "Love consists in this: not that we loved God, but that *He loved us and sent His Son to be the propitiation for our sins.* Dear friends, if God loved us in this way, we also must love one another."

- Romans 15:1-3 – "Now we who are strong have an obligation to bear the weaknesses of those without strength, and not to please ourselves. Each one of us must please his neighbor for his good, to build him up. *For even the Messiah did not please Himself.*"

- 1 Corinthians 10:24, 31-11:1 – "No one should seek his own good, but the good of the other person.... Therefore, whether you eat or drink, or whatever you do, do everything for God's glory. Give no offense to the Jews or the Greeks or the church of God, just as I also try to please all people in all things, not seeking my own profit, but the profit of many, so that they may be saved. Imitate me, *as I also imitate Christ.*"

- 2 Corinthians 8:9 "For *you know the grace of our Lord Jesus Christ*: Though He was rich, for your sake He became poor, so that by His poverty you might become rich."

Notice the similarities of the last verse with Philippians 2. The phrase "though He was rich" is parallel to "though being in very nature God," and "for your sake He became poor" is similar to "He made Himself nothing" and "He humbled Himself." We are called to adopt His selfless patterns of thinking, feeling, and acting.[8] Simply put, Jesus sacrificed Himself for *your* sake, therefore you must sacrifice yourself for the sake of others.

Notes

1. For more on this passage, see my *Theological Foundations for New Covenant Ethics* (Frederick, MD: New Covenant Media, 2013), 71-83.

2. I use the ESV here because for some reason the HCSB translates *hen phronountes* as "focusing on one goal," but having one mind is what the Spirit through Paul wrote.

3. The word "interests" is not in the original but added for our understanding. Literally, it is "Everyone should look out not only for his own." As Matt Chandler writes, "Let each of you look not only to his own house, job, money, family, and friends, but also to the house, job, money, family, and friends of others." Chandler, *To Live is Christ*, 75.

4. Clearly, there was disunity of some sort in the congregation. Contra Chandler, who writes that Philippians is the "only letter that we have in the Scriptures in which Paul is not trying to correct bad teaching or rebuke bad behavior." *To Live is Christ*, 14. Here, as well as in 4:1-3, we see the conflict within and there is clear conflict from without addressed in chapter 3:1-3.

5. For the life of me, I do not understand why English translations refuse to translate such phrases more consistently.

6. Chandler, *To Live is Christ*, 53.

7. Dietrich Bonhoeffer, *Life Together* (New York, NY: HarperOne, 1954), 90-109, quoted in Frank Thielman, *Philippians* (Grand Rapids, MI: Zondervan, 1995), 107.

8. Fowl, *Philippians*, 6.

The Christ Hymn

Make your own attitude that of Christ Jesus, who, existing in the form of God, did not consider equality with God as something to be used for His own advantage. Instead He emptied Himself by assuming the form of a slave, taking on the likeness of men. And when He had come as a man in His external form, He humbled Himself by becoming obedient to the point of death – even to death on a cross. For this reason God highly exalted Him and gave Him the name that is above every name, so that at the name of Jesus every knee will bow – of those who are in heaven and on earth and under the earth– and every tongue should confess that Jesus Christ is Lord, to the glory of God the Father. (Philippians 2:5-11)

This paragraph is "by any showing, one of the most remarkable passages in all of the New Testament," says N.T. Wright.[1] It is rich and full of gospel truth. In all likelihood, it is an early Christian hymn, as some translations show in their formatting of these verses. If so, it is doubly precious because it shows how the earliest Christians worshipped Jesus and what they believed about Him even before the NT was written.

Incarnation

God became a man – a truth that should never stop amazing us.

But it's not just amazing, it is revealing. It shows just how desperate our condition was that He had to become one of us to save us. And think of the OT storyline: Where is the faithful son of David? Where is the obedient king? God Himself had to come to redeem His people and to sit on the eternal throne.

A lot of ink has been spilled on the phrase "he emptied himself" (*ekenōsin*, 2:7). Many have argued that Jesus gave up at least some of His divine attributes. But the text itself tells us *how* He emptied Himself—by assuming the form of a slave and taking on the likeness of men. It was subtraction by addition. Take the example of a rental Corvette. The car is new and shiny when I leave the lot, but if I take it off-roading and cover it in mud, I haven't subtracted any of its inherent worth, but I have added a layer of filth, which hides its underlying glory. In that sense, it becomes less than it was by taking on an inherently less worthy form.

This is historic Christian teaching. In AD 451, the whole Church gathered in response to false doctrine and agreed on the Scripture's teaching on the person of Christ. The creed of Chalcedon reads:

> We, then, following the holy Fathers, all with one consent, teach men to confess one and the same Son, our Lord Jesus Christ, the same perfect in Godhead and also perfect in manhood; truly God and truly man, of a reasonable [rational] soul and body; consubstantial [co-essential] with the Father according to the Godhead, and consubstantial with us according to the Manhood; in all things like unto us, without sin; begotten before all ages of the Father according to the Godhead, and in these latter days, for us and for our salvation, born of the Virgin Mary, the Mother of God, according to the Manhood; one and the same Christ, Son, Lord, only begotten, to be acknowledged in two natures, inconfusedly, unchangeably, indivisibly, inseparably; the distinction of natures being by no means taken away by the union, but rather the property of each nature being preserved, and concurring in one Person and one Subsistence, not parted or divided into two persons, but one and the same Son, and only begotten, God

the Word, the Lord Jesus Christ; as the prophets from the beginning [have declared] concerning Him, and the Lord Jesus Christ Himself has taught us, and the Creed of the holy Fathers has handed down to us.

Jesus is two natures in one person. He was already in the form (*morphē*) of God, and then He took the form (*morphē*) of man. He didn't abuse His rights but emptied Himself. Here there is probably an allusion to Adam.[2] Recall that the serpent told Adam and Eve, "You will be like God" (Gen. 3:5). The first Adam grasped at equality with God for selfish reasons; the last Adam, Jesus, *was* equal with God but didn't hang on to that right.[3] Unlike Adam, He didn't use it for His own sake, but gave it up for the sake of others.

Humiliation

The cross was reserved by the Romans for insurrectionists or unmanageable slaves. It was considered so degrading that a Roman citizen could only be crucified for high treason. Cicero, a Roman philosopher from the second century, described crucifixion as "a most cruel and disgusting punishment," suggesting that "the very mention of the cross should be far removed not only from a Roman citizen's body, but from his mind, his eyes, his ears." It was the greatest humiliation possible in the first century,[4] which is why a *crucified* Messiah was a "stumbling block to Jews and foolishness to Greeks" (1 Cor. 1:23).

In our day, the cross has been domesticated.[5] We see crosses dangling from necks, printed on t-shirts, perched on top of buildings, and tattooed on biceps. But in the first century, it evoked horror. Its victims were beaten, flogged, and hung naked in humiliation to make a statement to the watching world—*Don't mess with Rome!* Fastened to the tree, they would wearily pull themselves up for a breath, alternating between agonizing pain in their spiked feet and agonizing pain in their spiked hands, as their muscles cramped and searing pain shot through their lacerated back moving up and down against the rough timber. They experienced severe blood loss, dehydration, decreased oxygen, and increased carbon dioxide, causing

acidic conditions in their tissues. Fluid built up in their lungs
until they could no longer breathe.

That is how Jesus died. For us. For our salvation! Which is
why Paul could say seemingly bizarre things like "I will never
boast about anything except the cross of our Lord Jesus Christ"
(Gal. 6:14), and "I resolved to know nothing while I was with you
except Jesus Christ and him crucified" (1 Cor. 2:2 NIV). He was
pierced for our transgressions.

The Son of God humbled Himself. He, who sustains all things by
the word of His power (Heb. 1:3), was grabbed with the Roman
hands that He formed. *He humbled Himself.* He was spat upon
by the saliva glands that He made. *He humbled Himself.* He
was nailed with metal He made, by hands He made, to a cross
cut from a tree that He spoke into existence.[6] *He humbled Himself.* Though He could've summoned an army of angels to
destroy His crucifiers, He stayed on the tree, naked and
writhing. *He humbled Himself.*

After it all, His bloated corpse hits the ground.[7] Blood splat-
ters. Dust spreads. The religious leaders are proud to
have stamped out another imposter, another false would-be
Messiah. They turn to Deuteronomy 21 and warn their children
that anyone who hangs on a tree is cursed by God. Roman
soldiers arrive home having eliminated another threat to the
Roman Empire, having strung him up as a sign to all who would
pass by—*Don't defy Rome or you will end up like this.* They wash
their hands and scrub away the blood of God's Son before
they eat, drink, wrestle with their kids, and go to bed. Mean-
while, Jesus' body lays in a dark cave. Silent. As Russell Moore
puts it, "If you'd been there to pull open his bruised eyelids,
matted together with mottled blood, you would have looked
into blank holes. If you'd lifted his arm, you would have felt
no resistance. You would have heard only the thud as it hit the
table when you let it go....But sometime before dawn on a Sunday morning, a spike-torn hand twitched. A blood-crusted eye-
lid opened. The breath of God came blowing into that cave, and
a new creation flashed into reality."[8]

Exaltation

"For this reason God highly exalted Him." *For this reason!* As we have seen, the Christian pattern is suffering *then* glory: power *in* weakness, victory *through* defeat, exaltation *after* crucifixion. As God promised long ago, the coming Child would crush the head of the serpent, but His heel would be bruised in the process (Gen. 3:15). He would defeat evil *through* suffering.

Jesus has been given the name above all names—*Lord* (*kyrios*). One day, everyone will bow before Him and confess His lordship. This does not mean there will be universal salvation, but universal confession as to who Jesus truly is. We either "repent and confess him by faith as Lord now, or we will confess him in shame and terror on the last day. But confess Him we will."[9] Our culture is sold on relativism, that something may be true for you but it doesn't have to be true for me. Sometimes folks will say, "I am glad Jesus *works* for others, but He doesn't do it for me." But truth is not determined by what you or I think. Every person will bow before Jesus and confess Him as Lord, whether He "worked" for them or not.

Christ's preeminence is God's plan for the world. The way we glorify the Father is by exalting His Son. That's why we are called to make much of Jesus, as other NT passages also teach:

> He made known to us the mystery of His will, according to His good pleasure that He planned in Him for the administration of the days of fulfillment – to bring everything together in the Messiah, both things in heaven and things on earth in Him. To sum up all things in Christ. (Eph. 1:9-10)
>
> He is the image of the invisible God, the firstborn over all creation. For everything was created by Him, in heaven and on earth, the visible and the invisible, whether thrones or dominions or rulers or authorities – all things have been created through Him and for Him. He is before all things, and by Him all things hold together. He is also the head of the body, the church; He is the beginning, the firstborn from the dead, so that He might come to have first place in everything. (Col. 1:15-18)

The OT also taught this, like Isaiah 45:22-25, which Paul quotes here in Philippians 2:

> *Turn to Me and be saved, all the ends of the earth. For I am God, and there is no other. By Myself I have sworn; Truth has gone from My mouth, a word that will not be revoked: Every knee will bow to Me, every tongue will swear allegiance. It will be said to Me: Righteousness and strength is only in the LORD. All who are enraged against Him will come to Him and be put to shame. All the descendants of Israel will be justified and find glory through the LORD.*

The apostle takes this Scripture asserting that there are no gods besides Yahweh and applies it to Jesus.[10] As Stott put it, Jesus is given a God title, a God text, anticipating God worship. Jesus is Lord! Worship Him!

Notes

1. N.T. Wright, *The Climax of the Covenant* (Minneapolis, MN: Fortress, 1993), 56.

2. For more allusions to Adam, see Wright, *The Climax of the Covenant*, 57-62. Also see James D.G. Dunn, *The Theology of Paul the Apostle* (Grand Rapids, MI: Eerdmans, 1998), 281-88. Dunn has a faulty Christology, but his observations here are helpful for non-heretics.

3. The HCSB, along with the NIV 2011, nails the translation of *harpagmos*. For the options, see Wright, *The Climax of the Covenant*, 62-90.

4. Fowl, *Philippians*, 99.

5. Carson, *Basics for Believers*, 46.

6. Chandler, *To Live is Christ*, 76.

7. This paragraph is adapted from Russell Moore, *Tempted and Tried* (Wheaton, IL: Crossway, 2011), 124-25.

8. Moore, *Tempted and Tried*, 125.

9. Carson, *Basics for Believers*, 48.

10. Interestingly, the same passage about YHWH in Isaiah is applied to God the Father by Paul in Romans 14:11-12.

Work Because God Works

So then, my dear friends, just as you have always obeyed, not only in my presence, but now even more in my absence, work out your own salvation with fear and trembling. For it is God who is working in you, enabling you both to desire and to work out His good purpose. Do everything without grumbling and arguing, so that you may be blameless and pure, children of God who are faultless in a crooked and perverted generation, among whom you shine like stars in the world. (Philippians 2:12-15)

Earning *No*, Effort *Yes*

The Christian life takes work. We are not saved *by* works, but we are saved *for* works (cf. Eph. 2:8-10). It's important to distinguish between effort and earning. We can never earn our way to God or earn God's favor, but we are called to exert effort after we have believed: "Therefore, brothers, make every effort to confirm your calling and election, because if you do these things you will never stumble. For in this way, entry into the eternal kingdom of our Lord and Savior Jesus Christ will be richly supplied to you" (2 Peter 1:10-11).

The Christian's work is to partner in the gospel of grace (Phil. 1:5, 7), to walk as a worthy citizen of the gospel (Phil. 1:27), and to love humbly and selflessly (Phil. 2:1-4). And we are to do these things in community. "Your" is plural, so it is not, "Work out your individual salvation," but, in good Texas form, "Y'all work out y'all's salvation." In this sense, our salvation should be a collaborative effort.

But are we really supposed to do this with fear and trembling? Non-Christians will face God on Judgment Day without a mediator or covering for their sin, but why should believers fear God? After all, 1 John 4:18 reads, "There is no fear in love; instead, perfect love drives out fear, because fear involves punishment." Christians do not fear God's judgment—there is no condemnation for those in Christ (Rom. 8:1)—but we do fear in the sense of being in awe of Him and revering Him. That is how we are to live out our saving faith.

Have you ever heard of myotonic goats, also known as fainting goats?[1] If not, stop reading this and Google it. After the Fall, many animals need some sort of defense mechanism to keep from being eaten. Porcupines are covered in needles. Some lizards shoot blood out of the eyes. Skunks dowse their would-be opponents with a spray that'll make them choke. Some birds regurgitate their lunch and projectile vomit on their enemies. The opossum plays dead. Some lizards poke their ribs through their skin to use as daggers. Pretty astounding stuff, really. But the myotonic goat has a rather ineffective defense mechanism. When scared, his leg muscles tighten up abruptly and become stiff as a board. Sometimes it's just the back legs, which is hilarious to watch, but usually it's all four, so of course the goat "faints." He falls flat on his side and ends up looking like an upside down stool. If you are in a pen with a myotonic goat, you aren't too worried. You might have contests with friends to see who can ground the goat the quickest. You might even consider getting myotonic goats as entertainment for your next men's retreat.

But what if you were in a pen with a full-grown *lion* rather than a goat? There is no creative scaring, no contests except to see who can get out of there the fastest. Instead, there is respect, awe, reverence. We are put in our proper place: *That is a lion and I am a man.* That is the sort of healthy reverence and fear we should have toward our Creator.

In the classic work by C. S. Lewis, *The Lion, the Witch and the Wardrobe*, the four children enter Narnia through a magic wardrobe. Three of the children go to the house of Mr. and Mrs. Beaver where they are told that they will soon meet the King—*Aslan*. The dialogue continues as follows:

> "Is – is he a man?" asked Lucy.
>
> "Aslan a man!" said Mr. Beaver sternly. "Certainly not. I tell you he is the King of the wood and the son of the great Emperor-Beyond-the-Sea. Don't you know who is the King of Beasts? Aslan is a lion, the Lion, the great Lion."
>
> "Ooh," said Susan, "I thought he was a man. Is he – quite safe? I shall feel rather nervous about meeting a lion."
>
> "That you will, dearie, and make no mistake," said Mrs. Beaver; "if there's anyone who can appear before Aslan without their knees knocking, they're either braver than most or else just silly."
>
> "Then he isn't safe?" said Lucy.
>
> "Safe?" said Mr. Beaver; "don't you hear what Mrs. Beaver tells you? Who said anything about safe? 'Course he isn't safe. But he's good. He's the king I tell you."

We are to work out our salvation with reverent fear before our great and holy King.

Work Out Your Salvation

As Carson points out, verse 13 is not saying, "Work to earn salvation because God has done His part." Neither is he saying, "You have started salvation and you must complete it." And it certainly does not say, "Let go and let God."[2] It says that we are to work because *God* works. Since He is actively moving our desires and deeds for His good purposes, we should pursue them, too.

The Scripture everywhere teaches that God is meticulously sovereign and people are fully responsible. These two biblical truths are compatible:

* *"You planned evil against me; God planned it for good." (Genesis 50:20)*

- *"A horse is prepared for the day of battle, but victory comes from the LORD." (Proverbs 21:31)*

- *"But by God's grace I am what I am, and His grace toward me was not ineffective. However, I worked more than any of them, yet not I, but God's grace that was with me." (1 Corinthians 15:10)*

Paul worked harder than all. But not really. God did. So how can we work alongside God? Just that, *work*. Pray for the desire; prayerfully work.

And without grumbling or arguing. Boy, we live in a grumbling culture, don't we? Just login to Facebook. It seems like many folks have their laptops open and ready all the time. As soon as they end a less than pleasant experience with some poor customer service rep trying to make ends meet, they run over and pound the keyboard in a rant. We are so ungrateful.

Technology has made us professional complainers. It used to be that if a person wanted to learn about car engines, he would have to drive to a store, browse through books until he found one on the right topic, buy it, drive home, and read it. Now, people complain because their computer or smart phone has a hiccup and takes four extra seconds to pull that book out of nowhere. I see this most clearly in airports. People love to complain about their negative airport experience. We bemoan a 30-minute delay rather than standing in awe of the fact that we were just flying with the eagles. We were strapped into a padded seat—in the *sky!*

What is grumbling, really? Is it not saying, "God doesn't know how to run this world?" We forget whose world this is and who we are.

Paul only uses *grumbling* one other time, referring to the Israelites in the wilderness (1 Cor. 10:10).[3] The book of Numbers uses it frequently. For example, in 14:27: "How long must I endure this evil community that keeps complaining about Me? I have heard the Israelites' complaints that they make against Me." When faced with opposition and hardship, the Israelites often complained and doubted God's goodness. We, the true Israel and the true circumcision, must be better than they were (see 1 Cor. 10:1-13). When faced with hardship and opposition, we must remember that God is at work. It has been granted to us

to believe *and to suffer* for His sake (Phil. 1:29). We have been
freed from slavery to Satan, sin, and death, but we have not yet
arrived at the Promised Land. We are still sojourners and aliens.
Our citizenship is not here but in Heaven (Phil. 3:20). We are
tempted to get frustrated, but we must not be like stiff-necked
Israel. Don't doubt God's leadership and purposes, even when
you don't see them.

Philippians 2:15 is soaked in Hebrew history. In a striking
manner, Paul describes the pagan world with the language used
of unfaithful Israel in Deuteronomy 32:5-6: "His people have
acted corruptly toward Him; this is their defect – they are not
His children but a devious and crooked generation. Is this how
you repay the LORD, you foolish and senseless people? Isn't He
your Father and Creator? Didn't He make you and sustain you?"
Israel was blemished (*mōmēta*), crooked and perverse (*skolias kai
destrammenēs*); the church is unblemished (*amōma*) in the midst
of a crooked and perverse generation (*skolias kai diestrammenēs*).[4]

Jesus said, "You are the light of the world. A city situated on a
hill cannot be hidden. No one lights a lamp and puts it under a
basket, but rather on a lampstand, and it gives light for all who
are in the house. In the same way, let your light shine before
men, so that they may see your good works and give glory to
your Father in heaven" (Matt. 5:14-16). We, as the New Covenant
community, are to be distinct from the world. Again, the Spirit
uses the language of Israel's calling. She was to be a light to the
nations (Isa. 42:6). Sadly, she ended up being like the nations
rather than a light to them. But the true circumcision, the true
kingdom of priests (1 Pet. 2:9), inherits the calling of Israel and
is faithful. We are called to shine, to stand out. If you don't complain and argue, you *will* stand out.

Notes

1. I owe this brilliant illustration to Chandler, *To Live is Christ*, 48-49.

2. Carson, *Basics for Believers*, 61.

3. Fowl, *Philippians*, 122.

4. See Frank Thielman, *Paul and the Law* (Downers Grove, IL: IVP, 1994),
    157.

10

Holding Firmly

Hold firmly to the message of life. Then I can boast in the day of Christ that I didn't run or labor for nothing. But even if I am poured out as a drink offering on the sacrifice and service of your faith, I am glad and rejoice with all of you. In the same way you should also be glad and rejoice with me. Now I hope in the Lord Jesus to send Timothy to you soon so that I also may be encouraged when I hear news about you. For I have no one else like-minded who will genuinely care about your interests; all seek their own interests, not those of Jesus Christ. But you know his proven character, because he has served with me in the gospel ministry like a son with a father. Therefore, I hope to send him as soon as I see how things go with me. I am convinced in the Lord that I myself will also come quickly. But I considered it necessary to send you Epaphroditus – my brother, coworker, and fellow soldier, as well as your messenger and minister to my need – since he has been longing for all of you and was distressed because you heard that he was sick. Indeed, he was so sick that he nearly died. However, God had mercy on him, and not only on him but also on me, so that I would not have one grief on top of another. For this reason, I am very eager to send him so that you may rejoice when you see him again and I may be less anxious. Therefore, welcome him in the Lord with all joy and hold men like him in honor, because he came close to death for the work of Christ, risk-

ing his life to make up what was lacking in your ministry to me.
(Philippians 2:16-30)

Life Eternal

The gospel is the *message of life*. It is the key to life now and the
way to gain life forever: "For God loved the world in this way:
He gave His One and Only Son, so that everyone who believes
in Him will not perish but have eternal life" (John 3:16). That
explains why Paul urges us to hold fast to it.

But what does that look like? Believing it, guarding it, defend-
ing it (Phil. 1:16), keeping it the main thing (1 Cor. 15:3), returning
to it again and again, and working for its advancement (Phil.
1:27). Because of the life promised in the gospel, Paul even
rejoiced in the possibility of dying. Death is the doorway to
Christ, which is far better than life here (Phil. 1:21-23). His mar-
tyrdom would simply be another way of offering a sacrifice to
God.[1] For this reason, and because he loved the Philippians, Paul
was happy and willing to die for their sake.

Life Examples

We have already seen many ways we can learn from Paul: he
cares for other believers (1:8), he prays for their spiritual growth
(1:9), he represented Christ in trials (1:12-13), he rejoices when
Christ is proclaimed (1:18), he is centered on Christ (1:20-21), he
is selfless (1:23-24), and, as we just saw, he is happy to die as a sacrifice for the benefit of the Philippians. Now we are told about
two other worthy examples to follow—Timothy and Epaphroditus.

Timothy is "like-minded," an allusion to the call to stand firm
and to be of one mind (Phil. 1:27; 2:2), and he is selfless, an allusion to the call to care for the interests of others rather than
for his own (Phil. 2:4). He has the Jesus mindset and cross-
shaped love. His value is not because he is a gifted leader, an
organized administrator, a dynamic communicator, or because
he has a history of success. No, he is valuable because he selflessly cares for the church. To love Christ is to love His body
(1 John 4:20-21). As one has put it, "To serve Jesus and to serve
his people are one and the same."[2] Timothy's character is

proven. Christian, find those people who have walked the walk, who are servants, who care about the advancement of the gospel and emulate them.

There is also Epaphroditus. Among other things, he is a "minister" (*leitourgos*), a word used in the OT to refer to the priestly work which took place in the temple.[3] The English word *liturgy* comes from it. In the Old Covenant, ministry occurred in a specific way in a specific place (cf. John 4:21-24). In the New Covenant, *minister* and *liturgy* refer to all of life. What was formerly *priestly religious service in the temple* is now *meeting the needs of other Christians*:

> "For the ministry of this service (leitourgias) is not only supplying the needs of the saints, but is also overflowing in many acts of thanksgiving to God." (2 Corinthians 9:12)

> "Yes, they were pleased, and indeed are indebted to them. For if the Gentiles have shared in their spiritual benefits, then they are obligated to minister (leitourgēsai) to Jews in material needs." (Romans 15:27)

> "Therefore, brothers, by the mercies of God, I urge you to present your bodies as a living sacrifice, holy and pleasing to God; this is your spiritual worship." (Romans 12:1)

Worship is not just an hour on Sunday morning.[4] It is our calling every day, all the time. The holy place is the marketplace. The sanctuary has been secularized.

Epaphroditus cares. He longs for other believers just like Paul does. And note the balance here about death (*"he was so sick that he nearly died"*). We saw in Philippians 1:21 that death is gain, but we also know that death is an enemy. Grief is real. Paul was not a stoic. Jesus Himself wept. There is pain and grief but there is hope in the midst of it. So imitate those believers who have persevered through hardship.

Good examples help us grow in the Christian life. Character is as much caught as taught,[5] and one of the main ways we learn to live Christianly is by observing mature Christians. We watch and absorb how they pray, how they read Scripture, how they lead, serve, and evaluate society. This is one of the reasons why intentional Christian fellowship is so essential. Imitate those who have adopted the mindset of Jesus and who risk their life for the sake of gospel advancement. Look for the Timothys and the Epaphrodituses. Be a Timothy! Be an Epaphroditus!

Notes

1. Cf. Exod. 29:38-42, Num. 15:5-7, 28:7.

2. Wright, *Paul for Everyone: The Prison Letters*, 110.

3. David Peterson, *Engaging with God* (Downers Grove, IL: IVP, 1992), 64, 183.

4. In the Bible, Sunday morning is primarily for edification. See David Peterson, *Engaging with God* (Downers Grove, IL: IVP, 1992). D.A. Carson defines worship as "the consistent offering of all of one's life and time and energy and body and resources to God; it is profound God-centeredness. There is a sense in which true Christians should never not be worshipping....Such a view of worship is not designed to depreciate what we do corporately on Sunday morning. It is designed, rather, to ensure that all of life is lived in faithful and delighted obedience to the gospel of God, with the result that what we do corporately when we come together on Sunday morning, or any other time, is the overflow of our experience of God and a place to be refreshed in the joy of the Lord as we think through his Word, express our praise and thanksgiving, and deepen our links of love with him and with one another. But the point to recognize is that under the terms of the new covenant, worship is bound up with all of life." (*Basics for Believers*, 77, 79.)

5. Carson, *Basics for Believers*, 69.

11

The True Circumcision

Finally, my brothers, rejoice in the Lord. To write to you again about this is no trouble for me and is a protection for you. Watch out for "dogs," watch out for evil workers, watch out for those who mutilate the flesh. For we are the circumcision, the ones who serve by the Spirit of God, boast in Christ Jesus, and do not put confidence in the flesh. (Philippians 3:1-3)

You may have heard of the little girl who asked her father, "Daddy, what does the preacher mean when he says 'finally'?" The dad responded, "Nothing, sweetie, he means nothing by it."[1] This paragraph begins with "Finally," but Paul, in typical preacher fashion, continues on for a couple of chapters before he wraps it up. Yet he does not apologize for repeating himself because he understands the necessity of constant reminders in the Christian life. Long ago, pastor-theologian Dietrich Bonhoeffer noted that normally you teach information previously unknown so that you don't have to teach it again: "It is of the essence of teaching that it seeks to render itself superfluous."[2] But not so with Christian truth. Repetition is the very thing it requires. Paul told Timothy to "keep reminding God's people of these things" (2 Tim. 2:14 NIV). We forget so easily. We need to hear truth again and again, which is one of the reasons we meet weekly.

It seems like Paul was going to close the letter but felt compelled to issue a warning. His tone changes—*Watch out! Beware of evil workers!* This language is reminiscent of John the Baptist calling the Pharisees a brood of vipers (Matt. 3:7), or Jesus calling them hypocrites and white-washed tombs (Matt. 23:27), or Paul calling for the damnation of false gospel preachers (Gal. 1:8), or his wishing that those who insist on circumcision would lop the whole thing off (Gal. 5:12). Paul is dead serious about false teaching and the purity of the gospel.

How serious are we? Today, it is unpopular to be so exclusive. Today, the only heresy is to believe in such a thing as heresy. Tolerance has been redefined. It used to mean that two people could disagree but still get along with one another, accepting that other viewpoints do exist even if you think they are wrong. In our postmodern culture, all views must be accepted (except the view that some views are not acceptable).[3]

In Greco-Roman society, dogs were despicable, unclean scavengers. First century Rome didn't have doggie hotels or doggie spas. Jews would often use "dog" as a term of derision for non-Jews. Even today, many Muslims are taught that they must perform a ritual purification if licked by a dog, and a dish licked by a dog must be cleansed seven times. So when Paul called these false teachers "dogs," it was a strong insult.

He also called them "evil workers." Why the harsh words? Because they wanted to add works to the gospel of salvation by faith. There is a word play here. He says beware the *katatōmē* for we are the *peritōmē*. Perhaps a better translation would be: Look out for the incision because we are the circumcision.[4] The Jews are a false circumcision, a "synagogue of Satan" (Rev. 2:9; 3:9) because they reject Jesus as Messiah. They are no longer worthy of the name "circumcision" or the title "Jews." Everywhere the apostle went, false missionaries followed seeking to distort the gospel. And nothing has changed. People are constantly adding to the sufficiency of Jesus, whether by imposing rules about homeschooling or forbidding dancing or endorsing political parties or any number of secondary issues. Christians must be on guard against the unclean intruders whose good works are actually evil.

In the OT, circumcision marked out Israel's uniqueness. As God's people, they were supposed to be a light to the nations, but they began to think they were superior, a "cut above," pun intended. The coming of Christ changed everything. Now, *Christians* are God's people. We inherit His promises. The New Covenant redefines who the "circumcision" is, and it's not about anything done to the foreskin of men.

God had promised long ago to circumcise the *hearts* of His people: "The LORD your God will circumcise your heart and the hearts of your descendants, and you will love Him with all your heart and all your soul so that you will live" (Deut. 30:6).[5] This was not speaking about the Jewish people, for they remained "circumcised yet uncircumcised," and "uncircumcised in heart" (Jer. 9:25-26). The promised "circumcision of the heart" was fulfilled by the outpouring of the Spirit at Pentecost. When anyone, Jew or Gentile, believes the gospel, he receives the new heart. Believers are the *Deuteronomy 30* people. Christians are the true circumcision, those who have the end-time gift of the Spirit and those who only boast in Jesus Christ. We are *true* Jews, those who have new hearts, just as Ezekiel promised long ago (Ezek. 36-37). Circumcision in the New Covenant has nothing to do with physical foreskin and everything to do with the heart.

The NT is univocal on this point, as we should expect, since there is ultimately one Author. Here are some examples:

According to John, the ethnic Jews by and large did not receive Jesus. But those who *did* receive Him were given the right to become *true* Jews, born not of blood or ethnicity, but of God (John 1:12-13).

"For a person is not a Jew who is one outwardly, and true circumcision is not something visible in the flesh. On the contrary, a person is a Jew who is one inwardly, and circumcision is of the heart – by the Spirit, not the letter. That man's praise is not from men but from God" (Romans 2:28-29).

Paul writes in Galatians: "Understand that those who have faith are Abraham's sons" (Gal. 3:7). The sons of Abraham (that is, *Israel*) are those who have faith in Jesus. He goes on to say, "For you are all sons of God through faith in Christ Jesus. For as many of you as have been baptized into Christ have put on Christ like a garment. There is no Jew or Greek, slave or free, male or female; for you are all one in Christ Jesus. And if you belong to Christ, then you are Abraham's seed, heirs according to the promise" (Gal. 3:26-29). In the new age, there is no distinction between Jew and Greek. All are one in Christ regardless of ethnicity. If you are "in Christ," Israel's Messiah, you are the seed of Abraham, heirs of the promise.

Paul concludes Galatians with: "Neither circumcision nor uncircumcision means anything; what counts is the new creation. Peace and mercy to all who follow this rule – to the Israel of God" (6:15-16 NIV). Ethnicity no longer matters. Being circumcised as a physical Jew is no longer the way to become Israel.

It's not that the Church has replaced Israel, but through Israel's Messiah the Church has *fulfilled* Israel. God promised that the offspring of Abraham would be as numerous as the stars of the sky. He was talking about *Christians*. Father Abraham has many sons – in Christ, I am one of them and so are you. Praise the Lord!

Starting in 3:3, we find the characteristics of the true Israel. *First*, she worships (*latreuō*).[6] "Worship" here means to perform religious rites, especially priestly duties. As we have seen, all Christians are priests in the New Covenant, which means we all have ministry to do, and it looks different for each of us.[7]

Second, she worships by the Spirit of God. The prophetic writings of the OT are filled with promises that God would give His Spirit to all of His people in the New Covenant. Those promises were fulfilled on the day of Pentecost. As Jesus told the Samaritan woman, worship would now be characterized by the Spirit and truth, rather than by a special location (John 4:19-24). The new Israel worships by the New Covenant gift of the Spirit (Rom. 7:6).

Third, she boasts in Jesus. The nature of the gospel is such that when you add to the work of Christ, you are actually taking away from the work of Christ. His work is finished. Once. For. All. He needs no supplement. He sat down when His work was done. We glory in the Lord and in the Lord alone. Jeremiah 9:23-24 says,

> *This is what the LORD says: The wise man must not boast in his wisdom; the strong man must not boast in his strength; the*

wealthy man must not boast in his wealth. But the one who boasts should boast in this, that he understands and knows Me – that I am the LORD, showing faithful love, justice, and righteousness on the earth, for I delight in these things. This is the LORD's declaration.

Paul picks up this passage in 1 Corinthians 1:28-31:

God has chosen what is insignificant and despised in the world – what is viewed as nothing – to bring to nothing what is viewed as something, so that no one can boast in His presence. But it is from Him that you are in Christ Jesus, who became God-given wisdom for us – our righteousness, sanctification, and redemption, in order that, as it is written: The one who boasts must boast in the Lord.

In Galatians 6:14, Paul says,

But as for me, I will never boast about anything except the cross of our Lord Jesus Christ. The world has been crucified to me through the cross, and I to the world.

God could not be clearer—there is *zero* room for human boasting. Jesus is our boast.

Fourth, she puts no confidence in the flesh. The flesh (*sarx*) is the tendency of fallen humanity to sin. One NT scholar defines it as "humanity in its fallen frailty, unable to help itself and in need of God's redemption."[8]

Paul often contrasts Spirit and flesh. Here are four key places where he does so:

- Romans 8:4-6 – "In order that the law's requirement would be accomplished in us who do not walk according to the flesh but according to the Spirit. For those who live according to the flesh think about the things of the flesh, but those who live according to the Spirit, about the things of the Spirit. For the mind-set of the flesh is death, but the mind-set of the Spirit is life and peace."

- Romans 8:9 – "You, however, are not in the flesh, but in the

Spirit, since the Spirit of God lives in you. But if anyone does not have the Spirit of Christ, he does not belong to Him."

- Galatians 3:3 – "Are you so foolish? After beginning with the Spirit, are you now going to be made complete by the flesh?"

- Galatians 5:16-17 – "I say then, walk by the Spirit and you will not carry out the desire of the flesh. For the flesh desires what is against the Spirit, and the Spirit desires what is against the flesh; these are opposed to each other, so that you don't do what you want."

Confidence in the flesh is confidence in the old age, in the old Adam. By effective grace, we have come to know that there is no room for boasting in and of ourselves. *Nothing in my hand I bring, simply to the cross I cling.* One of Augustine's favorite passages is also mine: "What do you have that you didn't receive? If, in fact, you did receive it, why do you boast as if you hadn't received it?" (1 Cor. 4:7). We are saved by grace through faith, and this is not from ourselves, it is God's gift "so that no one can boast" (Eph. 2:8-9). Confidence in Christ and confidence in self are mutually exclusive.[9] You cannot properly have both.

Notes

1. Carson, *Basics for Beleivers*, 80.

2. Dietrich Bonhoeffer, *The Cost of Discipleship* (New York, NY: Simon and Schuster, 1995), 249.

3. See D.A. Carson, *The Intolerance of Tolerance* (Grand Rapids, MI: Eerdmans, 2012).

4. N.T. Wright, *Paul and the Faithfulness of God* (Minneapolis, MN: Fortress Press, 2013), 986.

5. See also Deut. 10:16, Jer. 4:4, Ezek. 44:9.

6. The Holy Spirit used a similar word in a similar way in Philippians 2:25 where Epaphroditus "ministered" (*leitourgos*) to Paul's needs.

7. Ephesians 4:11-12 says that Jesus "personally gave some to be apostles, some prophets, some evangelists, some pastors and teachers, for the training of the saints in the work of ministry, to build up the body of Christ." Did you know that the work of ministry is primarily the responsibility of the church?

8. Thielman, *Philippians*, 176.
9. *Ibid*, 169.

12

Christ Is All

Although I once also had confidence in the flesh. If anyone else thinks he has grounds for confidence in the flesh, I have more: circumcised the eighth day; of the nation of Israel, of the tribe of Benjamin, a Hebrew born of Hebrews; regarding the law, a Pharisee; regarding zeal, persecuting the church; regarding the righteousness that is in the law, blameless. But everything that was a gain to me, I have considered to be a loss because of Christ. More than that, I also consider everything to be a loss in view of the surpassing value of knowing Christ Jesus my Lord. Because of Him I have suffered the loss of all things and consider them filth, so that I may gain Christ and be found in Him, not having a righteousness of my own from the law, but one that is through faith in Christ – the righteousness from God based on faith. My goal is to know Him and the power of His resurrection and the fellowship of His sufferings, being conformed to His death, assuming that I will somehow reach the resurrection from among the dead. (Philippians 3:4-11)

Paul's Extreme Makeover

There is no place for boasting in personal status or accomplishments, but if there were, Paul would be at the head of the line. He was circumcised properly, as the Law required (Gen. 17:12; Lev. 12:3). He could trace his lineage back to Abraham's grandson Benjamin, the only one of the twelve born in the Promised Land (Gen. 35:16-18).[1] He was Hebrew ethnically and probably read the Hebrew language. He was a Pharisee, the strictest of the Jewish sects (Acts 26:5), and so passionate for Judaism that he persecuted the Christian "sect" for their heresy. In Galatians 1:13-14, he writes,

> *For you have heard about my former way of life in Judaism: I persecuted God's church to an extreme degree and tried to destroy it. I advanced in Judaism beyond many contemporaries among my people, because I was extremely zealous for the traditions of my ancestors.*

He saw Christianity as a threat to the purity and integrity of Israel so he opposed it zealously and violently.[2] One NT scholar writes, "So Paul was fulfilling his obligation as a Pharisee to promote the Law and protect Israel from impurity by seeking to wipe out the new movement before it spread like cancer. He believed that this zeal, like that of Phinehas [see endnote 2], was the basis of his right relationship with God – his justification. But this violent and exclusivistic impulse would be challenged and, non-violently, overthrown."[3]

Outwardly, Paul was an extremely good example of one who kept Torah. He does not, of course, mean that he was sinless. The Law itself provided temporary atonement for sin through the sacrificial system. Also recall that this is one of the things in the list of what it means to have confidence in the flesh, which is not a good thing.[4] But he had a high sense of his own self-worth.

Until he discovered Christ. Then his evaluation changed.

The Bible uses the language of a ledger here. All that was in the credit column has been moved to the debit column. Now only Christ is in the credit column.[5] Christ is all. He is of surpassing value – which makes Paul's entire past a loss. It would be like you striving hard to get out of debt, working and saving and making weekly deposits, only to find out months later that you had actually been making withdrawals. In your heavenly bank account, none of your self-reformation projects count as a credit. Only Christ. All else is *skubala,* a very crude word

66

meaning: refuse, filth, excrement, rubbish, garbage, that which is thrown to the dogs.[6] The best translation is probably *crap*.[7]

What do you base your identity on? Where do you find your worth? On wealth? education? job? family? status? emotional stability? political alignments? business success?[8] Or is Jesus your constant boast?

Christian Righteousness

Paul's former problem, which is the problem of all mankind, was that God requires perfect righteousness. But no one is perfectly righteous. Trust in Jesus solves the problem by giving believers a righteous status before God.

Notice four things about this righteousness:

1. It is found "in Him."

All people are either *in Adam* or *in Christ*. Union with Christ is the key that unlocks the riches of Christ, the hub from which all the spokes of the blessing of salvation flow. Consider a few verses (with italics added to emphasize union with Christ):

- "They are justified freely by His grace through the redemption that is *in Christ Jesus*." (Romans 3:24)

- "Therefore, no condemnation now exists for those *in Christ Jesus*." (Romans 8:1)

- "But if, in our endeavor to be justified *in Christ*, we too were found to be sinners, is Christ then a servant of sin?" (Galatians 2:17 ESV)

- "For our sake he made him to be sin who knew no sin, so that *in him* we might become the righteousness of God." (2 Corinthians 5:21 ESV)

- "And because of him you are *in Christ Jesus*, who became to us wisdom from God, righteousness and sanctification and redemption." (1 Corinthians 1:30 ESV)

You get the picture. Righteous status is found in union with Christ. As Calvin said in the first paragraph of Book Three of *The Institutes*: "First, we must understand that as long as Christ remains outside of us, and we are separated from him, all that he has suffered and done for the salvation of the human race remains useless and of no value for us."[9]

2. It is not earned by our own Law-keeping.

Galatians 2:16 is emphatic in this regard: "Know that no one is justified by the works of the law but by faith in Jesus Christ. And we have believed in Christ Jesus so that we might be justified by faith in Christ and not by the works of the law, because by the works of the law no human being will be justified." Note that the apostle basically says the same thing three times in a row in this verse.

3. It comes through faith in Jesus Christ.[10]

Merely having *faith* is unacceptable to God. People today assume that as long as you believe something and are sincere about it, you are good with God. Sincerity is garbage to Paul. He was *sincerely* committed to Judaism, advancing beyond his peers, but he was sincerely *wrong*. Faith in Christ is the necessary and exclusive condition for being found righteous before a holy God.

4. It is a gift of God.

Oh, and what a precious gift! Infinitely more valuable than all the world's gold, the highest academic pedigree, and all the respect of all the businesses of the world. *Dressed in his righteousness alone, faultless to stand before the throne.* We needed an alien righteousness, one that we could not produce ourselves, and God, in His grace, has provided it. Praise Him!

Resurrection Hope for All

Paul was knocked off his horse 30 years prior to writing this letter, and it remained his profound passion to know Jesus. I wonder if this is true of us? Do we long to know Him? Does our passion grow as time moves on? We must know Him because *He* is eternal life (John 17:3), which begins now. The power of His resurrection is the power at work in us to transform us from self-consumed people into others-centered people, from being consumed with advancing our own kingdom to advancing the gospel of grace.

When Paul says that he wants to be conformed to Jesus' death, he doesn't mean Roman crucifixion, he means having the *Jesus mindset* of emptying himself for the sake of others and dying to self for the good of others. It is taking up our cross the way Jesus took up His. And Paul can thrive through this death because it leads to life. In fact, it is the only path to life. As C. S. Lewis noted, nothing not dead will be resurrected.[11] "If you want to get to the resurrection of the dead, this is the only way to go."[12]

This passage is helpful for non-Christians and Christians alike. For example, the unbeliever who thinks he is too bad for God to love him has that excuse pulled out from under him. Paul killed Christians! Our right standing comes through faith in Christ, not through what we have or have not done. The righteousness that counts before God is not our own, it is a gift from God.

We often hear testimonies about people leaving the garbage of immorality in order to find Christ. Like the guy who was beaten as a child, turned to drugs and alcohol, got locked up for burglary, was released, and amazingly left it all behind to follow Jesus. Praise God for such! But equally edifying are the testimonies of people leaving the garbage of *moralism*. How easily we adopt a Christianized view of Paul's former self-righteousness: "I was baptized (circumcised the eighth day), brought up in a Christian home (of the tribe of Benjamin), and taught all the right Bible answers (Hebrew of Hebrews)." I recall being very encouraged by a young man in our church whose testimony sounded like this: "Hi, my name is John. I grew up in church, never did drugs, am a virgin, and have always been a good kid. I now trust in Christ and want to be baptized." He traded the rubbish of personal righteousness for Christ's righteousness alone.

Others may think that they have no need of forgiveness because they are righteous *by comparison*. Measured next to other men and women, they conclude that they are okay without Christ. But we will always be able to find someone more crooked than we are. Even Ted Bundy could say, "I'm no Hitler." God sets the standard, and it is perfection. A man cannot be made right with God on his own. He will be saved in Christ's righteousness or be condemned in his own.

Notes

1. Fowl, *Philippians*, 150. Only Benjamin and Judah remained loyal to the line of David. Most Jews didn't even know to which tribe they belonged due to records being lost during their captivity.

2. "Zeal" alludes to Elijah and Phinehas. Phinehas in particular was probably Paul's hero before submitting to Christ. When the Israelites were worshipping idols supplied by Moabite women, Phinehas saw a man bringing a pagan woman into his tent, and he killed both of them with a spear – he is called "zealous" (Num. 25). First Maccabees narrates the story of an unfaithful Jew who made a sacrifice to a false god. When Mattathias saw it, he "burned with zeal and his heart was stirred. He gave vent to righteous anger; he ran and killed him upon the altar. At the same time he killed the king's officer who was forcing them to sacrifice, and he tore down the altar. Thus he burned with zeal for the law, *as Phinehas did against Zimri the son of Salu*" (1 Macc. 2:23-26, italics added). No doubt, Paul saw himself as standing on their shoulders when he violently protected the purity of Israel. See Michael Gorman, *Inhabiting the Cruciform God: Kenosis, Justification, and Theosis in Paul's Narrative Soteriology* (Grand Rapids, MI: Eerdmans, 2009), 129-60, and N.T. Wright, *What Saint Paul Really Said* (Grand Rapids, MI: Eerdmans, 1997), 26-29.

3. Michael Gorman, *Reading Paul* (Eugene, OR: Cascade, 2008), 14.

4. Stephen Westerholm, *Justification Reconsidered* (Grand Rapids, MI: Eerdmans, 2013), 41.

5. Carson, *Basics for Believers*, 84.

6. Fowl, *Philippians*, 153.

7. Richard B. Hays, *Echoes of Scripture in the Letters of Paul* (London: Yale, 1989), 122; N.T. Wright notes of this word, "Students usually enjoy being told, which is the truth, that the best translation of this is 'shit' or 'crap,' though the word can simply mean 'kitchen scraps' or 'garbage.'" *Justification* (Downers Grove, IL: IVP, 2009), 149.

8. Carson, *Basics for Believers*, 86.

9. John Calvin, *Institutes of the Christian Religion* Vol. 1, trans. Ford Lewis Battles, ed. John T. McNeill (Louisville, KY: Westminster John Knox Press, 2006), 3.1.1, 537.

10. I take the traditional objective genitive view. See Phil. 3:8, 10 with Christ as the object of knowledge.

11. C.S. Lewis, *Mere Christianity* (1952; Harper Collins: 2001) 223-225.

12. Wright, *Paul for Everyone: The Prison Letters*, 121.

13

Reaching Forward

Not that I have already reached the goal or am already fully mature, but I make every effort to take hold of it because I also have been taken hold of by Christ Jesus. Brothers, I do not consider myself to have taken hold of it. But one thing I do: Forgetting what is behind and reaching forward to what is ahead, I pursue as my goal the prize promised by God's heavenly call in Christ Jesus. Therefore, all who are mature should think this way. And if you think differently about anything, God will reveal this also to you. In any case, we should live up to whatever truth we have attained. Join in imitating me, brothers, and observe those who live according to the example you have in us. For I have often told you, and now say again with tears, that many live as enemies of the cross of Christ. Their end is destruction; their god is their stomach; their glory is in their shame. They are focused on earthly things, but our citizenship is in heaven, from which we also eagerly wait for a Savior, the Lord Jesus Christ. He will transform the body of our humble condition into the likeness of His glorious body, by the power that enables Him to subject everything to Himself. (Philippians 3:12-21)

As we have seen, imitation is a common theme in Paul's theology. In 1 Corinthians 11:1, he wrote, "Imitate me, as I also imitate Christ." Paul gave himself for the good of others, even when it would have been preferable to be with the Lord. Timothy and

Epaphroditus genuinely cared for the interest of others over their own. In this way, they imitated Jesus, the ultimate example of self-sacrifice and love. This is what it looks like for Christians to run the race and finish well.

Paul was an example worth following, but he readily acknowledged that he was still short of the goal. He hadn't *arrived*. (He says it twice in a row!) He was not yet fully mature. This is true of all of us. We are works in progress just as he was. And, like him, we are dependent on God's help to make it. Christ first takes hold of us, then we take hold of His promises.[1] This parallels Philippians 2:12-13 where we are told to work out our salvation because it is God at work in us. God's work is the ground for ours. To use the nomenclature of grammar, the indicative always grounds the imperative. The imperative is the fruit which flows from the indicative root.

Paul does not use his dependence on God's work as an excuse not to work hard himself. He is focused on "one thing," and he strains forward toward the goal. We should imitate his hard work. As Dallas Willard puts it, grace is not opposed to effort but to earning. The difference is vital. How much effort do you put into your Christian walk? Do you know those folks whose holiness is so above yours that it is just embarrassing? They didn't just wake up one day like that, they worked hard. In a growing Christian life, there is no sitting still, no microwave holiness, no cruise control. It's like Paul said in 1 Corinthians 9:24-27:

> *Don't you know that the runners in a stadium all race, but only one receives the prize? Run in such a way to win the prize. Now everyone who competes exercises self-control in everything. However, they do it to receive a crown that will fade away, but we a crown that will never fade away. Therefore I do not run like one who runs aimlessly or box like one beating the air. Instead, I discipline my body and bring it under strict control, so that after preaching to others, I myself will not be disqualified.*

God has given us a race to run. Friend, races are hard work. They require training, early hours, blood, and sweat. And they are not over until the finish line is reached. "Somehow" (Phil.

3:11), by whatever means necessary, we have to reach it. We have to persevere until we reach the resurrection.

Sanctification is a life-long, progressive process. You may have seen the bumper sticker that reads, "Christians aren't perfect, just forgiven." There is some truth to that, but we are much more than just forgiven. I think Paul's bumper sticker would say, "Christians aren't perfect, just forgiven and therefore striving for perfection." As D.A. Carson writes, "Paul cannot be satisfied with a brand of Christianity that is orthodox but dead, rich in the theory of justification but powerless when it comes to transforming people's lives."[2] So we need to consistently ask ourselves: *Am I making progress in the Christian life? Do I know His Word better and better? Is the fruit of the Spirit evident in my life?* Friend, if there is no progress, there is reason to doubt whether or not you are a genuine believer. Faith and repentance are two sides of the same coin. Where true faith is present, there will be turning away from sin to God. As Calvin put it, God has given every believer a race of repentance to run one's whole life. The goal is eternal fellowship with Christ Jesus in the resurrection.

Progress requires us to forget the past. How many Christians are hung up or bogged down by something that is behind them? Move forward! March on! And don't think that because of some past experience you are good. (*I am just fine. I made a decision for Jesus. I prayed the prayer. I signed the card.*) The real question is how are you running *now*? In high school, basketball was my idol. It was all I lived and breathed. I played it year-round. My junior year, the cross country coach apparently needed kids, so he recruited me. I agreed to run – with the sole purpose of getting in shape for basketball season. I came in about the time of the first mock race (the rest of the team had already been training for a month), and I'm not sure how, but I won. It went straight to my head. I decided I'd go ahead and *dominate* cross country. The next meet was our first real competition—three miles. I jumped out in the top five. Now I knew that these guys had run at the state meet the year before, but for some reason I thought I could hang. And hang I did, for the first two and a half miles, largely motivated by the folks who cheered louder than normal for me since I was new and no one expected to see me in fifth place. Needless to say, my adrenaline out-lasted my body. I don't really recall much after the first mile. I do remember seeing the finish line, but my legs simply would not keep going. They were burning incredibly and would not work any longer. I collapsed. People kept cheering me on, so I managed to crawl across the finish line, then immediately turned over and began to hyperventilate for what felt like an hour. After a trip to the ER and an IV, I was fine. (A friend later told me that towards the end I looked like a dog with parvo.) The point my race proved is – it does not matter how you start, it matters how you finish.

Remember Your Citizenship

Worldly people are driven by their appetites. Lacking all self-control, they continually feed their fleshly desires. They are focused on earthly things. Not us! Our citizenship is not of this world, but in Heaven. We are not Americans first, but Christians first. It is easy to forget this and merge the two. Citizenship confusion abounds. America is clearly not a Christian nation currently, and it is doubtful that it ever was. When people say they want America to return to its Christian roots, I always ask, "Which Christian roots?" Some of the first settlers believed that America was the new Canaan and that the Native Americans were the heathen to be killed and wiped off the land. Are those the roots we want to return to? Or how about when white Europeans enslaved millions of Africans because of skin pigment? Richard Hughes writes, "From Indian removal and extermination to African slavery to racial segregation to state-sanctioned killing in wars for dominance and profit to state-sanctioned torture of enemy combatants – in all these ways and more, Christian American has made a mockery of the Christian religion."[3] And there is the fact that many of the Founders were more deistic than Christian. John Adams was a Unitarian, denying the Trinity. Thomas Jefferson denied all the main doctrines of Christianity, but since he liked Jesus' moral teaching, he kept those parts of the NT and cut out all of the miracles and stuff he did not like. The Declaration of Independence proclaims truths thought to be "self-evident." In other words, they were based on *reason*, not *Revelation*. And when quoting verses like 2 Chronicles 7:13-14—"If I close the sky so there is no rain, or if I command the grasshopper to consume the land, or if I send pestilence on My people, and My people who are called by My name humble themselves, pray and seek My face, and turn from their evil ways, then I will hear from heaven, forgive their sin, and heal their land."— we should be careful to remember that they were not written about America. "My people" refers to Israel.

This is why I am partly uncomfortable with *U.S.* flags flying in the building where the *international* people of the Lord Jesus meet. It is not that I am unpatriotic, but I am more pro-Kingdom where nation-states matter not. As Preston Sprinkle put it, "Passports are irrelevant in God's kingdom."[4] Christians are to walk not (primarily) as worthy citizens of our particular nation-state but of the gospel because our citizenship is in Heaven. We have a distinct political identity which provides the focus for our allegiance and commitments.[5] As Wright puts it, "The task of the Roman citizen in a place like Philippi was to bring Roman culture and rule to northern Greece, to expand Roman influence there."[6] We are the colony of Heaven charged with the task (as we pray in the Lord's prayer) for bringing the life and rule of Heaven to bear on this earth.[7]

Hope in the Resurrection

The basic pledge of allegiance of the Roman world was "Caesar is Lord." So when the Christ hymn in Philippians 2:5-11 declares that every tongue will confess *"Jesus Christ* is Lord," the not-so-subtle implication is that Caesar is not. The emperor was also called a "savior," that is, one who delivers from adversity, whether it be material, spiritual, or military.[8] Being a Roman colony, the Philippians could call on their "lord" and "savior" at any time to come from the mother city and help them.[9] Therefore, when Paul spoke of awaiting a Savior from Heaven, he was using the sort of language the Philippians were familiar with. But Jesus is not merely the ruler of one temporary empire, He is the true Lord and Savior of the whole world.

And He will redeem the whole world (Rom. 8, Rev. 21-22). Contrary to evangelical pop theology, our ultimate hope is not Heaven, where soul is split from body, but resurrection, when soul and body are reunited on the new earth. That is why

Paul's goal is to reach the resurrection from the dead. God's grand plan moves from creation to new creation. One day, He will transform our bodies into the same glorious form as Jesus now has.

This hope helps us deal with suffering in this life. The pattern of Jesus' life—suffering, then glory—informs our life-pattern. Self-emptying humiliation and death came first, exaltation came second. "For this reason," God exalted Him (Phil. 2:9-11). The same goes with us: suffering followed by glory and exaltation. We do well not to try to reverse the order.

Notes

1. Mature thinkers will agree with this. In one of those uniquely Christian paradoxes, the mature (*teleioi* in 3:15) are those who realize they are not yet fully mature (*teteleiōmai* in 3:12).

2. D.A. Carson, *A Call to Spiritual Reformation* (Grand Rapids, MI: Baker Academic, 1992), 177.

3. Richard T. Hughes, *Christian America and the Kingdom of God* (Chicago, IL: University of Illinois Press, 2009), 4.

4. Preston Sprinkle, *Fight: A Christian Case for Nonviolence* (Colorado Springs, CO: David C. Cook, 2013), 153.

5. Fowl, *Philippians*, 173. Recall that the Spirit alludes to the wilderness generation in Philippians 2:14-15.

6. Wright, *The Prison Epistles*, 126.

7. Ibid.

8. Fowl, *Philippians*, 173-74.

9. N.T. Wright, *Paul* (Minneapolis, MN: Fortress Press, 2009), 72; idem., *Paul for Everyone*, 126.

14

Stand Firm, Stand Together

*So then, my brothers, you are dearly loved and longed for –
my joy and crown. In this manner stand firm in the Lord, dear
friends. I urge Euodia and I urge Syntyche to agree in the Lord.
Yes, I also ask you, true partner, to help these women who have
contended for the gospel at my side, along with Clement and the
rest of my coworkers whose names are in the book of life. Rejoice
in the Lord always. I will say it again: Rejoice! Let your gra-
ciousness be known to everyone. The Lord is near. Don't worry
about anything, but in everything, through prayer and petition
with thanksgiving, let your requests be made known to God. And
the peace of God, which surpasses every thought, will guard your
hearts and minds in Christ Jesus. (Philippians 4:1-7)*

Building on what he has been saying ("so then"), Paul exhorts
the church he loves to *stand firm.* The rest of our passage
explains how.

Stand Firm by Being United

There was conflict in the church at Philippi. I don't know about
you, but I am glad we have gotten to the place where conflict
no longer happens among believers. *Riiiigght!* No, we need this
word more than ever. We must agree in the Lord, we must have
the same mind. It's not that we must all fully agree on every

jot and tittle, but the Holy Spirit is "appealing for a mental attitude that adopts the same basic direction as other believers, the same fundamental aim, the same orientation and priorities – that is, a gospel orientation."[1] When we keep the main thing the main thing, we are like-minded, even if we differ on the smaller things. Major on the majors!

When there is a conflict, we need to have the maturity to sit down with open Bibles and prayerful attitudes. We need to work hard to find agreement "on the matters of greatest importance: the gospel, the Word of God, the glory of Christ, the good of God's people, the beauty of holiness, the ugliness of sin – especially your own sin."[2] We are a faith family. Bailing on our local church should be the last option.

The verb for "agree" (*phrōneō*) occurs ten times in these four chapters. Do you remember the "Jesus mindset?" Read again the rich Christ hymn:

> *Fulfill my joy by thinking the same way, having the same love, sharing the same feelings, focusing on one goal. Do nothing out of rivalry or conceit, but in humility consider others as more important than yourselves. Everyone should look out not only for his own interests, but also for the interests of others. Make your own attitude that of Christ Jesus, who, existing in the form of God, did not consider equality with God as something to be used for His own advantage. Instead He emptied Himself by assuming the form of a slave, taking on the likeness of men. And when He had come as a man in His external form, He humbled Himself by becoming obedient to the point of death– even to death on a cross. (Philippians 2:2-8)*

The family of God is called to have the same selfless love that Jesus adopted when He gave up His rights in order to serve others.[3]

And notice that Paul pleads with them to reconcile, he doesn't rebuke them. This letter was most likely sent to one of the overseers of the church (Phil. 1:1) who would in turn read the letter aloud. Paul encourages him to help mediate and to see the conflict come to a godly resolution.

I think one of our besetting sins in America, perhaps due to the number of churches available to choose from, is disunity. What a poor witness to the watching world. Did you know that Jesus prayed for you and me, that we would be unified? He prayed,

> *...not only for these, but also for those who believe in Me through their message. May they all be one, as You, Father, are in Me and I am in You. May they also be one in Us, so the world may believe You sent Me. I have given them the glory You have given Me. May they be one as We are one. I am in them and You are in Me. May they be made completely one, so the world may know You have sent Me and have loved them as You have loved Me. (John 17:20-23)*

All too often, when there is the slightest conflict or even perceived offense, people abandon their church. I am not saying it is always wrong to leave over conflict, but the mature thing to do is to go to a brother or sister and work it out. It requires a humble attitude, and it's not easy, but it's right. Remember, as a believer in the gospel, you are first *sinner*, then *sinned against*. Be the bigger person. Work toward a community of mutual love, forgiveness, and support. Stay. Pursue reconciliation. Don't just leave. Perhaps you need to call a former member and deal with some things. As someone has said, the Church is like Noah's ark full of animals—it sure stinks in there, but if you get out, you drown. You *need* a faith family to do life with.

Stand Firm by Rejoicing

Twice in this paragraph we are called to rejoice. And not merely to rejoice, but to rejoice *in the Lord*, which makes all the difference. Why? Just from this little letter, we know that God has begun a good work in us which He will finish, that He has given faith to us, that even our trials are opportunities to advance the gospel, that Jesus emptied Himself and died on the cross for our sake, that He has risen from the dead, that God is working in us to desire and to work for His good pleasure, that the worst thing that can happen to us – death – is actually the best thing that can happen to us, that we are declared righteous not by our works but by His grace, that Jesus has taken hold of us, and that He will come again and transform each of our bodies into a glorious one like His. It is truly embarrassing that we should have to be reminded to rejoice.[4]

The ultimate reason for rejoicing is never your current circumstances. They are like shifting sand: unreliable and fleeting; some good days, many bad; some good hours, many bad. But when your joy is grounded in Jesus the King, your feet are on solid rock. When you really understand and believe the gospel of grace, you can rejoice in all circumstances. When you truly grasp the depths of your sin and the heights of God's love for you in Christ, you have an indestructible foundation to stand on. You have, and will always have, what matters most: God's love and acceptance. This truth remains even when you are broken and bleeding from trial after trial.[5] Remember, Paul is writing this from a Roman prison![6] And do you recall what he did after being beaten and imprisoned in his first visit to the city of Philippi? He held had an all-night worship session. Why? Because the ground of his joy was Christ. That is why he, and we, can rejoice in the Lord *always*.

Do you lack joy? It may be because you are not pursuing Christ. Intimacy with the Lord takes work, as we have seen ("Work out your own salvation," Phil. 2:12; "Make every effort," Phil. 3:12). Is there sin in your life you need to turn from? Are you praying? Are you spending time in His Word? Daily? If not, don't expect to be joyful in the Lord.

Stand Firm by Being Worry-Free

It is hard not to be anxious today. Technology hasn't helped. We have instant access to all the problems of the world. (And isn't it always the problems that make the news?) There was a time not that long ago where people only worried about local matters because that is largely all they knew of. But our worries aren't limited to international issues, we have our own to deal with: bills, rattlesnakes and scorpions (in my part of the country), health care, stock markets, social security, family, cancer, boys (now that I have a daughter), thieves, and a host of other things. But God is sovereign and trustworthy. As J.D. Greear puts it, "Know that worry springs from not being convinced of a sovereign God's love for you. Worry disappears when you realize that God loves you unfailingly and will let nothing interrupt His plans for your good."[7]

Listen to the words of our sovereign King:

> This is why I tell you: Don't worry about your life, what you will eat or what you will drink; or about your body, what you will wear. Isn't life more than food and the body more than clothing? Look at the birds of the sky: They don't sow or reap or gather into barns, yet your heavenly Father feeds them. Aren't you worth more than they? Can any of you add a single cubit to his height by worrying? And why do you worry about clothes? Learn how the wildflowers of the field grow: they don't labor or spin thread. Yet I tell you that not even Solomon in all his splendor was adorned like one of these! If that's how God clothes the grass of the field, which is here today and thrown into the furnace tomorrow, won't He do much more for you – you of little faith? So don't worry, saying, 'What will we eat?' or 'What will we drink?' or 'What will we wear?' For the idolaters eagerly seek all these things, and your heavenly Father knows that you need them. But seek first the kingdom of God and His righteousness, and all these things will be provided for you. Therefore don't worry about tomorrow, because tomorrow will worry about itself. Each day has enough trouble of its own. (Matthew 6:25-34)

Augustine said that things like worry, fear, and depression are smoke from the fires rising from our idols.[8] In other words, follow the smoke and it will lead you to what is functioning as your god. If we replace the true God with an idol, worry is the result.

So are we to grit our teeth and resolve not to worry? No, then we'll end up worrying about not worrying.[9] How then? Through prayer. Don't worry, pray.

We rarely, if ever, spend time alone with God. When was the last time you spent an extended time in prayer about the things that are worrying you? And then we become overwhelmed and wonder where He is. Is it any surprise that that does not work? The way to be anxious about nothing is to be prayerful about everything. As one has put it, anxiety and a genuine prayer are more opposed to one another than water and fire.[10]

And we must pray with thanksgiving because He loves us, desires to hear us, and is pleased to provide. Praying this way brings a most pleasing result: peace. Matt Chandler writes, "Thanksgiving and worry can't occupy the same space. Thanksgiving is worry's kryptonite. You can't worry if you're giving thanks."[11] Or as Luther put it, pray and let God do the worrying.

Notes

1. Carson, *Basics for Believers*, 102.

2. Ibid., 103.

3. See my *The Imitation of Jesus* (Frederick, MD: New Covenant Media, 2014).

4. Carson, *Basics for Believers*, 104.

5. Cp. James 1:2-4. God loves you so much, He is so committed to having your heart, that He will send the storm to wipe out whatever it is that you are putting your joy in besides Him to teach you that He alone is the ground of rejoicing. As the song goes, He washed my eyes with tears that I might see. *Ibid., 105.*

6. J.D. Greear, *Gospel* (Nashville, TN: B&H Books, 2011), 81.

7. Ibid., 56.

8. Ibid., 75.

9. Carson, *Basics for Believers*, 111-12.

10. J.A. Bengal quoted in Carson, *Basics for Believers*, 112.

11. Chandler, *To Live is Christ*, 176.

15

The Mind, the Wallet, and True Contentment

Finally brothers, whatever is true, whatever is honorable, whatever is just, whatever is pure, whatever is lovely, whatever is commendable – if there is any moral excellence and if there is any praise – dwell on these things. Do what you have learned and received and heard and seen in me, and the God of peace will be with you. I rejoiced in the Lord greatly that once again you renewed your care for me. You were, in fact, concerned about me but lacked the opportunity to show it. I don't say this out of need, for I have learned to be content in whatever circumstances I am. I know both how to have a little, and I know how to have a lot. In any and all circumstances I have learned the secret of being content – whether well fed or hungry, whether in abundance or in need. I am able to do all things through Him who strengthens me. Still, you did well by sharing with me in my hardship. And you Philippians know that in the early days of the gospel, when I left Macedonia, no church shared with me in the matter of giving and receiving except you alone. For even in Thessalonica you sent gifts for my need several times. Not that I seek the gift, but I seek the profit that is increasing to your account. But I have received everything in full, and I have an abundance. I am fully supplied, having received from Epaphroditus what you provided – a fragrant offering, an acceptable sacrifice, pleasing to God. And my

God will supply all your needs according to His riches in glory
in Christ Jesus. Now to our God and Father be glory forever and
ever. Amen. Greet every saint in Christ Jesus. Those brothers who
are with me greet you. All the saints greet you, but especially those
from Caesar's household. The grace of the Lord Jesus Christ be
with your spirit. (Philippians 4:8-23)

We now come to the end of our journey. As we conclude, note three resolutions the New Covenant people of God should make.

1. Resolve to Dwell on the Excellent Things

Your mind is vitally important. It is where the battle starts (which is why Jesus traced murder to hate and adultery to lust[1]). As the saying goes, "You are what you think." Or, "You are not what you think you are, but what you think, you are." As a man thinks, so he is (Prov. 23:7). What we feed our minds is vital as well. Christians should mediate on "whatever is true, whatever is honorable, whatever is just, whatever is pure, whatever is lovely, whatever is commendable...."

Do you dwell on excellent things or do you fill your mind with all sorts of garbage? Do you have a filter for TV and movies? Is it a Christ-honoring filter? Do you have a time-limit? Parents, let me encourage you to restrict the amount of "screen time" your child receives. Nowadays, when my family goes to a restaurant, I kind of want to be like Jesus in the temple and go around knocking smartphones out of children's hands. Can they not sit without entertainment for fifteen minutes? I promise, it is okay if they get bored for a moment. It may even be good for them. The problem is that the vast majority of entertainment is godless, and it normalizes wickedness. It easily leads to worldliness.

We must fill our minds with excellent things, replacing the trash of the world with the Word of God. We must dwell on it, consider it, and meditate on it, which takes time, effort, and self-control. A three-minute "devotional" simply will not do. Satan wants us to find many things more pressing, yet dwelling on the Scripture is one of the major ways to defeat sin (Psa. 119:11).

2. Resolve to Be Generous for the Kingdom

The Philippian congregation had generously supported God's mission by supporting Paul (Phil. 4:10, 14-20). This caused him to rejoice, but not in the way we might think. He was thankful for God's work in them. He kept God as the focus. That is how we should encourage others.

Have you ever asked or heard others complain, "Why do pastors always talk about money?" Well, the simple answer is because the Bible does. Yes, there are those wretched prosperity preachers who love mammon more than their Maker and are constantly seeking to pad their pin-striped pockets. But if a pastor is going to be faithful to God's Word, he must talk about giving. It is not about money, but about the mission of God advancing.

Luther said there must be three conversions when one comes to Christ: the mind, the heart, and the wallet. Your checking account indicates where your allegiance lies. Statistics show that the average church member gives 2.5% of their income.[2] In 2002, Barna did a study and discovered that only 6% of so-called born again adults tithed.[3] This is a problem, and faithful preachers address it.

Notice that Paul does not seek their gift but the profit that is being stored up in their account. You see, the more you give, the more will be credited to you. As Jesus put it,

> *Don't collect for yourselves treasures on earth, where moth and rust destroy and where thieves break in and steal. But collect for yourselves treasures in heaven, where neither moth nor rust destroys, and where thieves don't break in and steal. For where your treasure is, there your heart will be also. (Matthew 6:19-21)*

As we give to the church, to the mission of God, and to needy brothers and sisters, we are storing up treasures in Heaven. The only money we will see again is what we give. We are often too short-sighted to truly believe this. As C.S. Lewis wrote, "If we consider the unblushing promises of reward and the staggering nature of the rewards promised in the Gospels, it would seem that our Lord finds our desires not too strong, but too weak. We are half-hearted creatures, fooling about with drink and sex and ambition when infinite joy is offered us, like an ignorant child who wants to go on making mud pies in a slum because he cannot imagine what is meant by the offer of a holiday at the sea. *We are far too easily pleased.*"[4] Store up treasures in Heaven.

Randy Alcorn writes,

> Five minutes after we die, it will be too late to go back and redo our lives. Gazing into the eyes of the Christ we treasure, we'll know exactly how we should have lived. God has given us his Word so we don't have to wait to die to find out how we should have lived. And he's given us his Spirit to empower us to live that way now. Ask yourself: Five minutes after I die, what will I wish I would have done with the money and possessions God entrusted to my care: What will I wish I'd given away while I still had the chance? When you've come up with an answer, why not do it now? Why shouldn't we spend the rest of our lives closing the gap between what we are doing and what we'll wish we would have done for his glory?[5]

Spend your money with the Judgment Seat in mind, so that Jesus will say to you, "Well done, My good and faithful servant."

A man visited a family, and there was a baby just having a fit, crying and belly-aching. He asked the mother what was wrong, and she said, "Oh, he's teething." Then the man noticed the father over at the table writing in his checkbook and bawling just like the baby. The man asked what was wrong with him, and she said, "Oh, he's tithing." Giving can be hard because it is a "sacrifice" (Phil. 4:18). As David Peterson puts it, "Sacrificial giving for gospel ministry is thus shown to be an expression of the worship pleasing to God under the new covenant."[6]

We can be generous for the kingdom of God because we know that He will supply all our needs according to His riches in glory in Christ Jesus. He owns the cattle on a thousand hills.

3. Resolve to Be Content in All Circumstances

Philippians 4:13 is one of the most popular "coffee cup" verses in the Bible. It is also one of the most abused verses because it is often yanked out of its context. The word "things" is not actually in the Greek. The new NIV is more accurate: "I can do all *this* through him who gives me strength" (italics added). When we look at the surrounding context to see what *this* is, we see that the focus is on contentment. That is not to say that Christ does not give us strength in other things, but an amazing fourth-quarter comeback is not what Paul has in mind here.

Paul would not be pleased with Joel Osteen's eisegesis of this passage:

> Most people tend to magnify their limitations. They focus on their shortcomings. But scripture makes it plain: all things are possible to those who believe. That's right! It is possible to see your dreams fulfilled. It is possible to overcome that obstacle. It is possible to climb to new heights. It is possible to embrace your destiny. You may not know how it will all take place. You may not have a plan, but all you have to know is that if God said you can...you can!"[7]

This is actually the opposite of what the verse means. Paul is not saying, "Dream bigger dreams," but "When your dreams are shattered and unfulfilled, you can endure through Christ." Matt Chandler writes:

> Do you see now how Philippians 4:13 is not about chasing your dreams, following your passion, pulling yourself up by your bootstraps, accomplishing anything you want with God's help? It is instead the testimony of those who have Christ and have found Him supremely valuable, joyous, and satisfying. In a life constantly marked by these extreme highs and lows, Paul has found the great constant security, the great centering hope: Jesus Christ himself.[8]

Contentment is a great challenge because America is constantly trying to sell us her dream. Capitalism runs on insatiable consumerism. Rodney Clapp writes, "The consumer is schooled in insatiability. He or she is never to be satisfied – at least not for long. The consumer is tutored that people basically consist of unmet needs that can be appeased by commodified goods and experiences."[9] And today we have more than ever, yet we are so discontent. Think of your kids at Christmas. You worked hard to buy that book, and they don't so much as look at the cover before they toss it aside, still half-wrapped, to see what's next.

This is no small thing. Greed is idolatry (Col. 3:5). Randy Alcorn writes:

> Mall window shoppers and catalog browsers should remind themselves that greed isn't a harmless pastime; it's a serious offense against God. Just as one who lusts is an adulterer (Matt. 5:28), and one who hates is a murderer (1 John 3:15), one who is greedy is an idolater (Col. 3:5). No sin is greater than worshiping false gods and thereby depreciating the only true God. The fact that idol worshipers may surround us doesn't reduce the seriousness of our offense.
>
> Greed violates the first commandment: "I am the LORD your God....You shall have no other gods before me" (Ex. 20:2-3). The eighth commandment prohibits stealing (Ex. 20:15), a product of greed. The tenth commandment forbids covetousness (Ex. 20:17). Remarkably, the ten great laws of God, written in stone, contain no fewer than three prohibitions against materialism.[10]

Luther said,

> Money is Satan's Scripture, through which he works in the world, just as God does everything through the true Scripture.[11]

We are bombarded with advertisements which no longer inform us about the goods being sold but offer an alternate vision of life. All the ingredients for revival are there. You have Hell (being fat, unpopular, defeated, bored, sad, etc.), salvation (the product itself), and testimonies ("You will be changed forever! Don't settle for less! Just try [blank] and see how your heart will be strangely warmed!"). But it's all *false* advertising, and we only harm ourselves when we listen to its lies.

Paul's secret to being content is to depend on Jesus. Isn't this what we saw in the last chapter? We have *Him*, we focus on *Him*, and come what may, we rejoice in *Him*. Again, Luther says, "What the Lord gives me I will gladly accept; what He does not give me, I can just as well do without. That is my motto, that I am satisfied with what I have. That is how I run the household."[12]

Habakkuk 3:17-19 says:

> *Though the fig tree does not bud and there is no fruit on the vines, though the olive crop fails and the fields produce no food, though there are no sheep in the pen and no cattle in the stalls, yet I will triumph in Yahweh; I will rejoice in the God of my salvation! Yahweh my Lord is my strength; He makes my feet like those of a deer and enables me to walk on mountain heights!*

Conclusion

Paul ends with a final message of hope. The Philippian Christians were being persecuted by the Roman empire. Paul himself was in a Roman prison, which is why he spoke about suffering, and why he called them to be counter-cultural, walking worthy – not of Rome – but of the gospel (Phil. 1:27), and why he reminded them that their true citizenship was in Heaven (Phil. 3:20). And yet, who sends their greetings? "Those from Caesar's household" (4:22). The gospel was invading the empire, and Paul wanted them to draw encouragement from this to stay faithful.

Jesus wins! Therefore, they (and we) must resolve to dwell on the excellent things, to be generous for the Kingdom, and to be content in the Lord regardless of circumstance, all for His glory.

SOLI DEO GLORIA

Notes

1. Ibid., 115.
2. Ronald J. Sider, *The Scandal of the Evangelical Conscience* (Grand Rapids, MI: Baker Books, 2005), 20.
3. Ibid., 21.
4. C.S. Lewis, *The Weight of Glory* (New York, NY: HarperOne, 2009), 26.

5. Randy Alcorn, "Dethroning Money to Treasure Christ Above All" in *For the Fame of God's Name*, ed. Justin Taylor and Sam Storms (Wheaton, IL: Crossway, 2010), 327.

6. David Peterson, *Engaging with God: A Biblical Theology of Worship* (Downers Grove, IL: IVP, 1992), 184.

7. Today's Word with Joel Osteen – January 21, 2013. http://www.freerepublic.com/focus/ f-religion/2980275/posts. Accessed 4/30/14.

8. Chandler, *To Live is Christ*, 202.

9. Rodney Clapp, quoted in Skye Jethani, *The Divine Commodity* (Grand Rapids, MI: Zondervan, 2009), 108.

10. Randy Alcorn, "Dethroning Money to Treasure Christ Above All," 315.

11. Martin Luther in *Off the Record with Martin Luther*, ed. Charles Daudert (Kalamazoo, MI: Hansa-Hewlett, 2009), 97.

12. Luther, *Off the Record*, 97.

Other Books by Cross to Crown Ministries

Exalted by Douglas Goodin
God's Design for Marriage by Douglas Goodin
Bitter Truth by Linda R. Graf
Woman of Grace by Anne Brown

At *Cross to Crown Ministries*, our motivation is simple. We want to encourage believers to live purposefully with explicit devotion to Jesus Christ in every facet of life. This includes Bible study, teaching, marriage, parenting, worship, working, playing, learning, retirement planning, or anything else we do. To accomplish this task we are committed to:

- training pastors who interpret the Word of God from an intentionally Christ-centered perspective
- training elders to shepherd the Lord's people toward intentionally Christ-exalting living
- training lay leaders to direct church ministries according to intentionally Christ-focused purposes
- helping all students of the Scripture to intentionally read the Bible as the story of Jesus Christ
- creating resources that exalt Christ and encourage believers to be intentionally Christ-obsessed in all things

There are several distinct facets to our ministry. The *New*

Covenant School of Theology trains pastors, elders, lay leaders, and any interested Christian from the Christ-centered perspectives of New Covenant Theology and Biblical Theology. We also produce resources——written, audio, and video—to help you think and live intentionally Christianly. We hold conferences to bring Christians together for intensive Christ-centered preaching and teaching. We produce music to be used for personal and public worship and edification in the hope that our intentionally Christ-exalting, New Covenant-oriented songs will spur Christians to love and good deeds for His glory and praise. Our website (www.crosstocrown.org) is the one-stop location for all of our ministries and resources.

Made in the USA
San Bernardino, CA
16 November 2015